HOARD OF THE DRAGON QUEEN

By Wolfgang Baur and Steve Winter

TYRANNY of DRAGONS

CREDITS

KOBOLD PRESS

Designers: Wolfgang Baur, Steve Winter
Editor: Miranda Horner
Interior Illustrators: Aaron Hübrich, Tyler Jacobson, Guido Kuip, Marcel Mercado, Bryan Syme
Cartographer: Jared Blando
Art Director: Marc Radle
Producer: Wolfgang Baur

WIZARDS OF THE COAST

D&D Lead Designers: Mike Mearls, Jeremy Crawford
Producer: Greg Bilsland
Adventure Contributors: Mike Mearls, Christopher Perkins, Matthew Sernett, Chris Sims, Rodney Thompson
Art Directors: Kate Irwin, Shauna Narciso
Cover Illustrator: Raymond Swanland
Graphic Designers: Bree Heiss, Emi Tanji
Project Management: Neil Shinkle, John Hay
Production Services: Cynda Callaway, Jefferson Dunlap, David Gershman
Brand and Marketing: Nathan Stewart, Liz Schuh, Chris Lindsay, Shelly Mazzanoble, Hilary Ross, Laura Tommervik, Kim Lundstrom, Trevor Kidd

Playtesters: Melissa Bassett, André Bégin, Mik Calow, Mélanie Côté, Manon Crevier, Ben Danderson, Dave Eadie, Frank Foulis, Rodrigo Gorgulho, Pete Griffith, Liam Gulliver, Jon Harvill, Joseph Kauffmann, Yan Lacharité, Renata Landim, Rodrigo Landim, Éric Leroux, Carlos Eduardo Lopes, Julia Lopes, David Muller, Claudio Pozas, Paula Pozas, Count Response, Sara Servin, Robin Stacey, Jaime Thayer, Keoki Young

Disclaimer: The following adventure contains chromatic dragons. Wizards of the Coast cannot be held liable for characters who are incinerated, dissolved, frozen, poisoned, or electrocuted.

FOREWORD

You hold in your hands the inaugural campaign for the fifth edition of DUNGEONS & DRAGONS. With Wolfgang Baur and Steve Winter at the reins, you are in good hands. They both have long, storied histories with D&D. *Hoard of the Dragon Queen* reflects not only their vivid imagination and compelling adventure design skills but also their ability to juggle this project with an ever-evolving set of core rules. The D&D design team is indebted to them for their patience, ingenuity, and hard work in creating such a great campaign under tough circumstances.

Speaking of those core rules, you need only the basic rules and the *Tyranny of Dragons* online appendix to play through both this adventure and its sequel, *The Rise of Tiamat*. Both the rules and the appendix can be downloaded for free at DungeonsandDragons.com.

With laurels placed where they belong and the resources you need to enjoy this campaign at your fin-gertips, proceed. Good luck, and good (dragon) hunting!

Mike Mearls
May 2014

ON THE COVER

In this glacial scene illustrated by Raymond Swanland, the white dragon Glazhael takes ice sculpture to extremes, turning intruders into grisly decorations for its draconic lair.

620A9606000001 EN
ISBN: 978-0-7869-6564-9
First Printing: August 2014

9 8   (includes corrections)

CE

CONTENTS

TARBAW NIGHTHILL

THE SWORD COAST

INTRODUCTION

Tyranny of Dragons is an epic story told across two adventure products, of which this is the first. Characters begin at 1st level, and by the end of *Hoard of the Dragon Queen*, they should be 7th or 8th level and ready to continue with *The Rise of Tiamat*. The ideal party size is four characters. If your group is larger or smaller, you can adjust the adventure's difficulty by reducing or increasing the number of enemies present in a given encounter.

Tyranny of Dragons is set in the Forgotten Realms on Faerûn's western shore—the Sword Coast. A thin strip of civilization stretches down this coast, where widely spaced cities are arranged like beads on a string. A combination of roads and wagon tracks loosely connect the cities that stretch from Luskan in the north to Calimport in the south, passing through Neverwinter, Waterdeep, Baldur's Gate, and other great ports along the way. The bulk of this adventure takes place on the stretch between Baldur's Gate and Neverwinter.

Adventure Supplements. You can play this adventure with just the DUNGEONS & DRAGONS basic rules and the *Tyranny of Dragons* appendix online, which contains all the monsters and magic items not described in this book. Both of these supplements are available as free downloads on DungeonsandDragons.com.

Character Advancement. At your option, you can use the milestone experience rule. Under this rule, you pick certain events in the campaign that cause the characters to level up. In *Hoard of the Dragon Queen*, the characters gain a level after completing each episode except episode 5.

BACKGROUND

The Cult of the Dragon has been active in Faerûn for centuries. It has focused on making undead dragons to fulfill a prophecy most of that time, but that's changing.

DRAGON MASKS

The new leader of the cult is a Calishite named Severin Silrajin, who believes that real draconic knowledge and power belongs to living dragons, not undead ones. Severin's ambition amused Tiamat, so she revealed the existence of five dragon masks to him—one for each chromatic dragon color. Individually, these ancient masks allow wearers to communicate with dragons. More importantly, a person who is erudite in draconic lore becomes a wyrmspeaker while wearing the mask, which allows the wearer to think like a dragon, gain favor among dragons, and subtly influence their behavior. When all five are brought together, they magically merge into a single *Mask of the Dragon Queen*. With the assembled mask, the cult can release Tiamat from her prison in the Nine Hells.

After Severin (subtly guided by Tiamat) discovered that secret, he bent all the cult's resources to finding the long-lost dragon masks in their secret hiding places. When he recovered the red mask, Severin became the first of the wyrmspeakers, but others soon followed.

SECRETS

The Cult of the Dragon has kept secret its goal to bring Tiamat into the world thus far. Many know of the cult's increased activity along the Sword Coast, especially in the north, but the reasons behind the resurgence are unknown.

Besides his cultists, Severin has forged an alliance with a splinter faction of the Red Wizards of Thay. This small and secretive group, led by an outcast named Rath Modar, plots to unseat the lich Szass Tam from his position over the Red Wizards. Rath believes that in exchange for his help in releasing Tiamat, she will grant him the power he needs to overthrow Szass Tam.

CULT ORGANIZATION

The Cult of the Dragon is organized in cells, which vary in size from just a handful of members to scores. Leaders in the cult are known as Wearers of Purple, and they outrank normal cultists, but no formal grades exist within the ranks of the Wearers of Purple.

Although the cult uses regalia in its rituals and its distant camps, members who operate in public places dress and act no differently from anyone else.

The cult is not above hiring mercenaries when it has special jobs to fulfill. Indeed, many of the "cultists" that characters encounter in the first three episodes of this adventure are working for pay.

OVERVIEW

During the time covered by the first half of this adventure, the cult already has several of the five dragon masks. While the cult works to gain more, Severin initiates the second part of his plan to release Tiamat: recruiting dragons and assembling a treasure hoard worthy of the queen of evil dragons. These efforts draw the characters' attention to the cult.

The action begins when a town comes under attack by a dragon and its allies. Characters can intervene to save townsfolk, but not before attackers carry away an important scholar. While rescuing that captive from the raiders' camp, characters learn they are up against the Cult of the Dragon, and they have the chance to destroy a subterranean dragon hatchery that the cult guards.

The hatchery provides clues to the cult's operation and sends the characters on a long journey northward. During that trip, they face threats from the cult and gain some unexpected allies within the Zhentarim, a shadowy organization with an unsavory history. North of Waterdeep, the cult's contraband is offloaded at a smuggler's den for shipment to a castle long ago abandoned.

A portal beneath the temple connects to the stronghold of one of the cult's most powerful and most disgruntled members, Talis the White, who can become either a deadly enemy or a crucial collaborator to the characters. With or without Talis's help, the characters must get into a flying citadel that a cloud giant placed at the cult's disposal and prevent it from reaching its destination at the Well of Dragons.

EPISODE 1: GREENEST IN FLAMES

The town of Greenest was founded by the halfling Dharva Scatterheart, a rogue who fancied herself the queen of the Greenfields. Scatterheart passed away without ever achieving that level of eminence, but her town grew into a thriving community. Its success isn't surprising, since Greenest is the only town of any size astride the Uldoon Trail, the most direct road between the eastern cities of the Dragon Coast, Cormyr, and Sembia with the Coast Way running south to the great cities of Amn, Tethyr, and far Calimshan. The trade caravans that pass through Greenest bring gold to the town's merchants and craftsfolk, and Governor Nighthill runs the town at the behest of the inhabitants.

The adventurers might be on the road from one town to another or returning to their homes after a trip away. Alternatively, they could be accompanying a merchant or wealthy traveler as bodyguards. Many restless young people of Faerûn have had their first taste of travel and adventure as caravan guards.

You can adapt *Tyranny of Dragons* to different regions of the Realms or to a different setting with a bit more preparation on your part. Change the names and locations to suit your campaign.

CHARACTER HOOKS

To tie the characters' backstories to the *Tyranny of Dragons* campaign more closely, see appendix A.

THE APPROACH

As characters approach Greenest, they see that a blue dragon and its Cult of the Dragon allies are attacking the town. The cultists seek to collect treasure that they hope to present to Tiamat upon her arrival in the world. The cult has assembled a powerful force for this raid by gathering bandits, kobolds, sellswords, and other mercenary types into a small army. A monk named Leosin Erlanthar was also in town. Through diligent research and interviews conducted during his travels between Berdusk and Candlekeep, Leosin became convinced that the cult is engaged in a big operation, but he doesn't yet know what it is. Leosin uses the raid as an opportunity to infiltrate the cult so that he can learn more about the cult's plans. He is discovered and captured, however, and needs the characters' help to escape from captivity.

Characters can engage in several encounters while cultists and kobolds rampage through Greenest.

For the past several days, you have been traveling a road that winds lazily across the rolling grasslands of the Greenfields. Sundown is approaching when you top a rise and see the town of Greenest just a few short miles away. But instead of the pleasant, welcoming town you expected, you see columns of black smoke rising from burning buildings, running figures that are little more than dots at this distance, and a dark, winged shape wheeling low over the keep that rises above the center of the town. Greenest is being attacked by a dragon!

The sequence of events that follow is up to you and the characters. You can present them with as many of the encounters as you want, in any order. The only exception is "Seek the Keep," which should be the first encounter after characters enter Greenest.

General Features

The sun has set by the time characters reach the edge of town (the area shown on the Greenest map).

Light. Burning buildings and a half moon provide dim light throughout the town. The inside of the keep is brightly illuminated.

Fires. The cultists tried to set buildings ablaze as they moved through town, but thatch isn't as flammable as it looks. When characters arrive, most of the flames come from haystacks and barns, not from homes or shops.

The Stream. The stream that flows past Greenest is shallow (seldom more than 3 feet deep) with a gravel bottom, so characters can move along it without difficulty. Where the banks are clear, the stream is easy to get into or out of. Brush by the stream is dense, and the banks are steep where brush grows. Characters can move only 5 feet per turn through the brush.

Important Characters

Governor Nighthill. The man who runs Greenest is Tarbaw Nighthill, a human male of sixty years. If characters ask who's in charge, they are directed to Nighthill. He is pacing atop the parapet of the keep when the sky is clear, or inside the keep if the dragon is attacking. If the characters don't seek out the governor when they reach the keep, he finds them. Either way, Nighthill welcomes them and takes them to the parapet. From there, they have the best view of Greenest.

The right side of Nighthill's face and head are bandaged, his right arm hangs in a sling, and his light blue tunic is stained with his own blood. He received these

> ### Stolen Treasure
> The cultists and their kobold lackeys are in the midst of looting Greenest and collecting the spoils for transport back to their camp (see episode 2). Any marauding group that the party encounters has a 50 percent chance of having stolen treasure in its possession. Roll a d6 and multiply the result by 10 to determine the total value of the stolen items, in gold pieces (gp).

wounds during the early stages of the attack and hasn't spared the time for more than cursory first aid.

Castellan Escobert the Red. Escobert is a shield dwarf with knotted, tangled, bright red hair. As master of the keep, Escobert is in charge of its defense and is the best source of information on the tunnel and the sally port (see "The Old Tunnel" and "The Sally Port" below). He carries an enormous ring of iron and brass keys to the many locks in the keep.

Wandering Encounters

The streets of Greenest are overrun by forces consisting of **cultists** and **acolytes** accompanied by monstrous allies: **kobolds** with **ambush drakes** (see appendix B) and **giant lizards**. These raiders move through town without fear, pillaging as they go. As characters travel through the embattled village, they can run into raiders and townsfolk. Use these guidelines to determine if characters have an encounter.

If characters use cover and stealth to avoid encounters, have each character attempt a DC 10 Dexterity (Stealth) check. For every two individual checks that fail, the characters have one encounter on the way to their destination. Roll a d8 on the Episode 1 Encounters table to determine each encounter. If characters use the stream bed for cover for most of the trip, these characters have advantage on their Dexterity checks.

If characters don't use cover and stealth to avoid encounters, roll a d8 for every 100 feet they move in town. If the roll is 4 or lower, they didn't attract attention with that move. If the roll is 5 or higher, they run into something; roll a d8 again and check the Episode 1 Encounters table to see what the characters meet.

Episode 1 Encounters

d8	Encounter
1	6 kobolds
2	3 kobolds and 1 ambush drake (see appendix B)
3	6 cultists
4	4 cultists and 1 guard
5	2 cultists and 1 acolyte*
6	3 guards and 1 acolyte*
7	1d6 townsfolk being hunted by raiders (roll a d6 to determine the raiding group)
8	1d6 townsfolk hiding

* Acolytes have *command* prepared instead of *sanctuary*.

Most of the cultists, guards, and acolytes are human. At your option, you can include a few dwarves, half-elves, half-orcs, or halflings without altering any game statistics.

Seek the Keep

Characters have random encounters with raiders when they enter Greenest, but this one should be their first mission of the episode. It begins when a terrified human family (father, mother, and three young children) dash across their path, hounded by eight **kobolds**.

Without warning, five humans dash out from between two buildings on your left. A limping man and three young children race across the street into more shadows, and a woman carrying a round shield and a broken spear turns and faces back in the direction from which they came. Eight kobolds stream out of the alley on the family's heels and fan out around the woman, who looks determined to delay the creatures for as long as possible.

The woman is Linan Swift, and her husband is Cuth. Linan is a **commoner** but with 8 hit points. Her attack with the spear is +2 to hit for 1d6 piercing damage. Her husband is down to 2 hit points from an earlier fight. The children move at speed 20. They can be carried, but a character carrying a child has disadvantage on attack rolls and cannot wield a two-handed weapon.

Unless characters interfere, the kobolds assume the characters are cultists and ignore them to concentrate on killing the woman first, her family second. Assuming characters intervene and save the family, Linan explains that they must make their way to the keep (at area 1); it's the only safe place in Greenest. The raiders haven't set up an effective cordon around the keep, so it's still possible to move through the front gate—but not for long.

To reach the keep, the characters must make it past three groups of raiders. A group consists of 1d6 **kobolds** and 1d4 **cultists**. If the group contains six kobolds, one is a **winged kobold (urd)**.

Characters can fight these enemies, sneak past them, retreat to avoid them entirely, or try something clever such as bluffing. If they fight, run the combat normally. When enemies must make a check to notice sneaking or bluffing, make a check with advantage for the group.

Each time the characters retreat from an enemy group to avoid it, they run into d6 more townsfolk who are trying to reach the keep. For every four additional townsfolk in tow, the group must move past one more enemy group to reach the keep.

At the keep, the characters are the last group through the gate before it is closed and barred. After characters enter the keep, raiders encircle it in increasing numbers.

Rewards. Besides earning experience points (XP) for raiders fought on the way to the keep, characters earn a bonus of 50 XP per nonplayer character (NPC) brought alive into the keep. Divide this bonus equally among the party members.

MISSIONS

Events in Greenest are divided into missions. Missions don't need to involve combat, but most do.

The characters reach the town at sundown, or about 9 p.m. The sun comes up again at 6 a.m. the next morning, but the last of the raiders are gone by 4 a.m.

For time-keeping purposes, assume that each mission takes an hour. Time during the hour that isn't spent fighting or slipping through town is spent tending gear, bandaging minor wounds, patrolling the keep's walls, briefing Nighthill on the situation, and other mundane tasks. If characters take a short rest, they can't undertake any other mission that hour.

If players need guidance, Governor Nighthill can give the characters a quick briefing on the tactical situation. The raiders have isolated the keep from the town with encircling groups of guards, but they haven't organized an attack. Nighthill thinks the raiders don't intend to attack the keep; they seem interested only in loot. The real danger is to the town and to those people who didn't make it into the keep before it was cut off. Nighthill wants the characters to slip back into the town and help people who are cut off or harass the raiders. A stealthy group can make it out of the keep and back in again without drawing the raiders' attention.

THE OLD TUNNEL

A narrow tunnel runs from the cellar beneath the keep to the bank of the stream (area 2). The tunnel is wide enough to allow warriors to pass through it in single file. In the keep, the tunnel is sealed with a locked ironbound door, and the stream exit is covered with a locked iron grate made to look like a sewer outlet. The tunnel's main function was as a secret means of collecting water from the stream during a siege, but it can double as a sally port. Since the keep has never been besieged, the old tunnel has never been used. Barrels and crates are piled in front of the door. The keys for the locks are on the ring that Escobert carries with him everywhere.

At some point, Escobert recommends the tunnel as a means of sneaking townsfolk into the keep without running the gauntlet of attackers watching the gates.

Locks. Characters can clear the cellar door with a few minutes' work. The lock is stiff but opens with the key; without the key, the character can open the lock with a successful DC 10 Dexterity check and a set of thieves' tools. The disused tunnel is choked with webs but is otherwise clear. A few yards inside the stream end is a nest of two **swarms of rats**. The rats attack when disturbed, and the surviving rats flee when half their number die.

Years of exposure and neglect have corroded the lock on the exit grate. Even with the key, a successful DC 10 Dexterity check is needed to open the lock. Without the key, the DC increases to 20. If the roll misses by 5 or more, the key or thieves' tools break off in the lock so that unlocking it becomes impossible. Then only a successful DC 15 Strength check can force the grate open.

Foes. A group of cultists is searching the stream banks for hiding townsfolk when the characters emerge from the tunnel. If characters open the lock with the key or with thieves' tools, the first one to exit notices the raiders approaching without being spotted in return; the characters can keep out of sight in the tunnel or try to ambush the raiders after they pass. If the check fails, the raiders spot the character; roll initiative and proceed with combat. If the grate had to be broken open with a Strength check, the raiders hear the noise and find cover; they wait for the characters to exit the tunnel, then gain a surprise round. The raiders' group consists of two **cultists** and six **kobolds**. If any cultists are still alive at the beginning of the fourth round of the fight, one of them runs to fetch help. Ten minutes later, two **cultists**, ten **kobolds**, and one **ambush drake** (see appendix B) arrive to guard the tunnel.

Rewards. Award standard XP for defeated foes. Aside from that, the chief reward for this mission is the tunnel itself. As long as it remains secret, characters can use it to enter and exit the keep safely. Each time they use the tunnel exit, roll a d6. On a roll of 1, raiders see and attack the characters (use the Episode 1 Encounters table). On a roll of 2, they are seen but not attacked. Instead, the raiders set an ambush and attack the next time the characters return to the tunnel exit.

THE SALLY PORT

The keep has a sally port along the west wall for counterattacking foes who bring a battering ram against the gates. During the night while characters are in the keep, raiders approach the old gate, force it open, and rush through. Escobert discovers them and races into the courtyard to sound the alarm ahead of the infiltrators.

Enough defenders are available to deal with the immediate threat from raiders loose in the keep, since it's more a probe that got out of hand rather than a full-scale assault. Escobert is most concerned about resealing the sally port, and he seeks out the characters for that job.

To secure the sally port, characters must battle through two groups of foes. The first fight occurs against one **acolyte**, four **kobolds**, and one **ambush drake** (see appendix B), which are guarding the sally port's 10-foot-by-20-foot ready room against exactly this type of counterattack. After characters seize the room, they discover that the door is heavily damaged. The fastest repair is with five castings of *mending* (taking five minutes). If none of the characters can do this, an NPC in the keep knows the cantrip. Someone must find and fetch her to the ready room.

Before the door can be repaired, a second group of raiders consisting of one **guard**, three **cultists**, and four **kobolds** attacks. These foes can come from outside the keep, or they might be a group of infiltrators trying to fight its way back outside. If characters barricade the door with barrels or other heavy objects while awaiting repairs, they might hold off attackers until the repairs are finished and avoid this fight entirely.

Rewards. Award standard XP for defeated foes.

DRAGON ATTACK

The **adult blue dragon** Lennithon accompanied this raid but is not an enthusiastic participant. His chief contribution has been his Frightful Presence, but that becomes less effective as the night wears on and defenders overcome their fear. Shortly before midnight, the dragon launches a final assault against the citadel. Frulam Mondath orders the attack, knowing that the adventurers are in the keep at the time. Lennithon doesn't consider this to be his fight, and he isn't keen on tangling with adventurers for another's benefit.

During this attack, Lennithon flies over the keep and uses his breath weapon without moving closer than 25 feet from the parapet. The defenders on the walls have mastered their fear of the dragon's Frightful Presence from earlier attacks. There are twenty NPC defenders on the walls at the beginning of the mission, and more can arrive between attacks to take the place of those who fall. The dragon doesn't target the adventures at first, and every breath attack not directed at them kills 1d4 NPC defenders and injures 1d6 more. Adventurers who happen to get caught in the area make normal saving throws and take standard damage. The NPCs' attacks are ineffective against Lennithon. Bear in mind that the dragon's breath weapon will kill a 1st-level character outright, so be sure to demonstrate its destructive power to the players before turning the dragon against the party.

After each attack, Lennithon swoops away until his breath weapon recharges, then swings in for another attack. He repeats this pattern until he has taken 24 damage or more, or a single critical hit. After that happens, Lennithon leaves for good.

Rewards. Characters earn 50 XP each for driving away Lennithon, but reduce that award to 25 XP if 10 or more defenders were killed during the attack.

PRISONERS

Governor Nighthill would like to interrogate some of the raiders.

> "I'd give anything to know what we're up against, and why. For that, we need prisoners. A commander, even a low-ranking one, is best."

If the characters haven't run into any cult leaders yet, Nighthill takes them onto the parapet and points out what he means. This is an ideal time for everyone to catch a glimpse of **Frulam Mondath** (see appendix B) in her purple robes, accompanied by a dozen guards. Even the governor cautions characters against attacking such a formidable force, especially when any lower-level officer can answer his questions.

Leaving the keep through the front gate is out of the question. By now, too many raiders are watching it, and they would jump the characters as soon as they moved away from the keep. Other options are waiting for a cloud to cover the moon before climbing down ropes tossed over the back wall of the keep, or using the old tunnel that exits into the stream bed.

This mission can be combined with another mission, such as saving the mill or rescuing villagers from the temple of Chauntea. All characters need to do is bring a live cultist or Cult of the Dragon initiate back to the keep. Or characters can go into the town hunting for one specifically.

Prisoners brought back to the keep are interrogated by Governor Nighthill and a few of his picked guards. Characters can participate if they want to.

- Captured kobolds are terrified; they say whatever they think the questioner wants to hear. They know that

GREENEST

N
BLANDO

100 FEET   200   300

they're working for the Cult of the Dragon and for the "dragon lady" (Rezmir), and that they're after loot.

- Captured mercenaries or bandits talk freely; they have no special loyalty to the Cult of the Dragon. They reveal that they've been raiding communities around the Greenfields for loot, and they've heard rumors in the camp about dragon eggs.

- Cultists and initiates are the most tight-lipped. A successful DC 10 Charisma (Intimidation) or DC 12 Charisma (Persuasion) check is needed to cause cultists to reveal that they are members of the Cult of the Dragon and that they are collecting loot "for the great hoard that will usher in the reign of the Queen of Dragons." They know that the cult has a clutch of dragon eggs under heavy guard in a cave at the camp.

Rewards. If characters capture a prisoner, award each of them 25 XP. To collect that award, the prisoner must be brought to the governor. Interrogating the prisoner independently and bringing the information to the governor doesn't count. The characters also receive standard XP for any monsters they defeat along the way.

SAVE THE MILL

From the parapet of the keep, someone spots a group of raiders trying to set fire to the town mill (area 4). Governor Nighthill quickly approaches the adventurers.

"The guards have spotted a new threat. Raiders are trying to set fire to the town's mill. If it burns, we'll lose our stockpile of flour and we won't be able to grind more for months. I'm trying to assemble enough defenders from here in the keep to defend it through the rest of the night, but that will take time. You'd do us a great service if you could get to the mill quickly and drive away the raiders before they can set it aflame. You'll need to defend it until our force arrives to take over, but it shouldn't be more than fifteen minutes behind you."

The mill is about 500 feet from the keep. The distance is doubled if characters use the secret tunnel and follow the stream to stay hidden.

Roll a d6 on the Episode 1 Encounters table to determine the strength of the raiders that are trying to set fire to the mill. Any kobolds in this force run away as soon as two or more raiders are killed. If characters observe the mill for a minute or more before attacking, allow them to attempt DC 15 Wisdom (Insight) or Charisma (Performance) checks. If successful, a character realizes that the raiders are making a demonstration of starting a fire, but it's for show. A few fires are burning around the building, but they could be extinguished easily.

This act of burning the mill is a ruse. Mondath has been informed that heroes are aiding the town, and she wants to lure them into an ambush. More raiders—one

cultist plus one **guard** per character—are hiding inside the mill, waiting for the characters to show up.

The mill is a simple rectangular barn, about 40 feet long and 20 feet wide, with an attached, exterior office. The long side of the building away from the stream has barn doors and a two-part door, and the two short walls have windows. All these openings are closed, but none are locked or barred. Inside, the main floor is dominated by a massive stone grinding wheel driven by a water wheel in the stream. The mill was operating late when the raid began and the millers fled without disengaging the wheel, so it still turns noisily. The upper half of the barn is a loft where milled flour is stored. The loft can be reached by wooden stairs along the east wall or by using the ropes and pulleys that hoist bags of flour up and down through large openings in the loft floor.

The ambushers are waiting in the loft for heroes to enter the mill. When the heroes are inside, the guards launch a volley of spears from above, then leap down to fight hand-to-hand. The ambushers have a good chance to gain a surprise round for their spear volley; a successful DC 20 Wisdom (Perception) check is needed to notice them before the attack. Characters who scan the loft for hidden enemies upon entering the mill have advantage on the check.

Ten minutes after the second fight ends, a dozen bloody but basically healthy defenders arrive from the keep with orders to relieve the characters and defend the mill. They tell the characters to go back to the keep quietly while they remain behind at the mill.

Rewards. Award standard XP for defeated foes. If characters realized they were walking into a trap, give each a 50 XP bonus. If they didn't deduce that it was a trap but spotted the ambushers in time to prevent a surprise round, give each character a 25 XP bonus.

Sanctuary

Dozens of townsfolk have barricaded themselves inside the temple to Chauntea (area 3), which is surrounded by raiders. The attackers tried setting fire to the stout structure but had little success. Now they've deployed an improvised battering ram. It's only a matter of time, possibly minutes, before the temple's main doors crumple under the assault, leaving the people inside helpless.

The temple is a large building, made of fieldstone with a peaked slate roof, and square in shape. It is taller than most other buildings in town. Inside, the altar occupies the middle of the temple, with other worship areas arranged around it.

Foes. The force outside the temple is split into three groups. One (A) is battering at the front doors, another (B) is circling the temple in a screeching mob, and the third (C) is heaping burning straw against a rear door. All these groups together would overwhelm 1st-level characters, but characters can devise a plan that gets them inside the temple by dealing with one group.

Group A consists of one **dragonclaw** (see appendix B), two **cultists**, and six **kobolds**. The cultists are handling the ram while the kobolds stand guard in case the town militia mounts a counterattack. The dragonclaw is in charge. The kobold guards are alert, but they are distracted when Group B passes in front of the temple.

Group B consists of three **cultists**, ten **kobolds**, and two **ambush drakes** (see appendix B) strung out in a mob that stretches 50 feet. This procession with leaping and whirling kobolds completes one circuit around the temple approximately every eight minutes (two minutes per side).

Group C consists of two **cultists** and six **kobolds** clustered tightly around the temple's back door. Their meager fire produces little flame, instead creating prodigious clouds of thick smoke that engulf the back of the temple and blanket the surrounding 30 feet of ground. Everything in the smoke is lightly obscured, and objects or creatures that are seen through more than 15 feet of smoke are heavily obscured. Characters can sneak up on these raiders and gain a surprise round against them, as long as they avoid Group B in the process.

Arranging a Rescue. The heroes' best shot at rescuing the townsfolk is to overpower Group C and take control of the back door. In the temple, they can arrange a distraction to keep Groups A and B occupied at the front while the citizens of Greenest slip out the back and race for the keep or for the old tunnel—if characters have opened it already. That's only one possibility; clever players can come up with different solutions.

The townsfolk in the temple are near panic, however, and they won't take orders from strangers unless someone makes a successful DC 15 Charisma (Persuasion) check. Otherwise, characters need to locate the priest of Chauntea, Eadyan Falconmoon, a level-headed half-elf. He's easy to spot, being the only calm person they can find in the temple, and he is elated to see them. He looks to the characters for a plan.

Time is pressing. While characters are inside the temple, remind them of the booming hammer blows of the battering ram against the front doors, the cracking timbers, the stones and sputtering torches that fly through the windows intermittently, the smoke rolling below the ceiling, and the frightened townsfolk. How much time you allow before the doors burst open depends on your group; slow thinkers and careful plotters need more time than fast movers. What's important is that players feel pressed.

To create a sense of pressure, give the front doors 30 hit points and let each thud of the battering ram deal 1d6 damage. When the doors reach 20 hit points, they have cracks large enough to see through. At 10 hit points, the doors are sagging in their hinges. At 5, they could collapse at the next impact. How frequently you roll the die is up to you! One roll every 15–20 seconds is a good target for an average group. One roll every 30 seconds might be better for a group that needs to debate and reach consensus, while a group containing quick-on-their-feet, take-charge types could deal with a roll every 10 seconds. Be flexible, keep an eye on the players' level of tension, and don't let anyone relax.

If the doors burst open before the temple is evacuated, this scene turns into an ugly melee against Group A. The kobolds in that group prefer to attack unarmed villagers instead of lethal adventurers. Each kobold automatically kills one villager each round unless characters attack the kobolds, cut them off from their victims, or interfere some other way. If townsfolk have already evacuated the temple through the back door, or that process is well along before the front doors split apart under the ram, then characters can conduct a fighting withdrawal through the temple. After everyone gets into the smoke outside, they can close and brace the back door, then sprint for the keep or the tunnel in the stream bank with enough of a head start to get away safely.

Rewards. Rescuing people from the temple earns each character 100 XP in addition to the points for killing monsters. If more than ten villagers died during the rescue, reduce that award to 50 XP.

HALF-DRAGON CHAMPION

Before all the raiders depart, their champion challenges the town's best warrior.

> From the darkness, a creature strides into the dim light of the dying fires around the keep. Although it is shaped roughly like a human, it is at least seven feet tall, its skin is covered in blue scales, its fingers bear wicked claws, and its face has the muzzle and reptilian eyes of a dragon. The creature stops about eighty yards from the main gate of the keep and scans the walls. A line of kobolds fans out behind it. With their spears, they prod four human prisoners into the dim light. You can make out a woman, a teenage boy in a blood-soaked tunic, and two children. Then the half-dragon creature hails the keep.
>
> "Defenders of Greenest! This has been a successful night, and I am feeling generous. Do you see these four pitiful, useless prisoners? We have no need for them, so I will trade them back to you. Send out your best warrior to fight me, and you can have these four in exchange."

The speaker is **Langdedrosa Cyanwrath** (see appendix B for statistics) a half-blue dragon who serves the Cult of the Dragon. Cyanwrath has a personal troop of sixteen **kobolds**. A character who makes a successful DC 15 Intelligence (Arcana) or Intelligence (Nature) check recognizes the creature as a half-dragon from descriptions.

One of the defenders in the keep, Sergeant Markguth, recognizes the prisoners as his sister and her children, and he is ready to rush out into battle with the half-dragon. Escobert the Red and a few other defenders restrain him while Nighthill approaches the characters.

> "My friends, you've demonstrated your prowess all through this frightful night. I realize this is an awful burden to ask you to bear, but any of you has a better chance to defeat that horror than my militia have."

If no one steps forward, Nighthill is disappointed but says he understands, and their refusal in no way diminishes what they've done so far. In that case, the woman's brother goes out to face the half-dragon. He is a human **guard**. Select one of the players to control Sergeant Markguth for this fight or just narrate its result.

Cyanwrath is pleased to see a champion step forward. He agrees to these terms for the combat: The three children will be set loose immediately, but his kobolds will continue to stand guard over the woman, and they will kill her if anyone interferes in the fight—for example, if archers in the keep let fly at him. Regardless of who wins, the woman will be released when the fight is over; and the victor will be the last one standing.

Governor Nighthill holds his troops in the keep during the combat. Adventurers can go out if they want, but the half-dragon insists that they keep their distance and stay between him and the fortress. If characters try to surround him or to edge into position for an ambush, he warns them that his kobolds won't hesitate to kill the hostages if they see signs of treachery. The half-dragon is evil, but he has a deep sense of honor about one-on-one combat. He doesn't intend any shenanigans, and he won't allow any from his kobolds.

Cyanwrath is the likely winner of this match, whether he's fighting Sergeant Markguth or a character. When his foe drops, he strikes one more time; the last blow kills Markguth or inflicts one death roll failure on a character. If Cyanwrath loses the fight, the kobolds immediately jump in to protect his body and carry it away. (Cyanwrath will recover from his wounds and be encountered again later.) If by some mischance Cyanwrath is killed or captured, his place in the dragon hatchery (episode 3) is taken by another half-dragon.

With the fight over, the last of the raiders retreat en masse from the town into the darkness, marching away toward the southeast.

Rewards. If a character steps up to the challenge and fights Cyanwrath, each party member earns 50 XP. If not, characters receive nothing for this encounter. A team of healers with healer's kits and +4 bonuses to Wisdom (Medicine) checks attend to the wounded or dying character, and Governor Nighthill gratefully offers two *potions of healing* to the wounded character. If characters do something that costs the life of a hostage, Governor Nighthill is furious with them and offers no more help.

DEVELOPMENTS

It's assumed that when characters first see the fighting in Greenest, they will rush to its defense. If they don't, and they're traveling with others, then the NPCs they're traveling with suggest that an immediate attack might turn the tide or at least save many lives. If characters still sit out this fight, they see about half of the attackers leave around midnight, with the rest retiring in small groups over the next few hours. When the sun comes up, even a quick inspection shows that over half of the buildings are heavily damaged and much of the town's wealth was carried away. Hundreds of injured people are crowded into the keep or are found hiding in cellars, but most of them will survive.

If you are using the milestone experience rule, the characters reach 2nd level at the end of this episode.

EPISODE 2: RAIDERS' CAMP

In the warm light of day, Governor Nighthill and other leaders want to know who was behind the attack on Greenest, and why the town was a target. The raiders retreated toward the southeast, and their trail is easy to spot. A small, stealthy group could follow the trail to the raiders' camp and gather information.

Governor Nighthill approaches the characters with a proposal: If they locate the raiders' camp and find out certain information, he offers to pay them 250 gp apiece. He wants to know where the camp is sited, how many raiders are there, who their leaders are, what's motivating these attacks, and where they plan to strike next. If characters recover valuables that were stolen from the town, he would like them returned, but he does his best to arrange a reward from what's left of the town treasury. Recovering treasure, however, is a lesser goal when compared to the other objectives he brings up.

Any gear or supplies the characters need for the trip are furnished by the town. As characters prepare to set off on this mission (or to leave town if they turn down the mission), though, an injured monk approaches.

A young man walks up to you, limping heavily on his bandaged left leg. "I hear that you intend to follow the raiders and see where they've gone. I'd like nothing better than to come with you, but in this condition, I'd slow you down. In the midst of all this tragedy, there's no reason you would have heard about the fate of my master, Leosin Erlanthar, but it's important you know. He is a monk from Berdusk. He disappeared last night, after we fought a particularly savage battle against raiders. A few others and I fought our way to the keep, barely. Leosin didn't make it at all. We went back this morning to look for him, but all we found was his broken staff and this choker, which he always wore."

The monk's name is Nesim Waladra. After introductions are made, he continues.

"Leosin has been investigating these raiders for months. I fear that he might have tried to infiltrate their group when they retreated, or worse, was captured and carried away as a prisoner. No one understands these bandits better than he does, and his knowledge will be invaluable against them. When you find their camp, please look for any sign that Leosin is there. One of my brothers has already departed for Berdusk to bring back help, but it will be many days before help arrives. Anything you can do before then would be a godsend."

Nesim answers the characters' questions to the best of his ability, but he also urges them to move quickly. The monks were returning to Berdusk from the great library at Candlekeep, where Leosin was consulting the librarians and researching ancient writings on dragon folklore. Dragon cults are his special interest.

The broken staff is nothing special. The choker is a braided leather neckband with a silver dragon design chased into the leather. The ends are ragged, as if it was roughly torn off.

Tracking the Raiders

The raiders' path is easy to follow across the rolling grassland of the Greenfields. A wide swath of grass is trampled down, but it's impossible to determine the raiders' numbers precisely. The path only confirms what characters already know: there were a lot of them, and they were a mix of humans, kobolds, and trained reptiles. One bit of information can be gleaned with a successful DC 15 Wisdom (Perception) check: Many of the beasts' footprints are deeper on the retreat than they were on the approach march. They were weighed down with loot on the homeward-bound trip, but let players reach that conclusion on their own. It's not possible to tell from the confusing jumble of prints whether any specific footprints are those of prisoners.

Cult of the Dragon Ranks

The Cult of the Dragon has an active recruiting process, accepting initiates from a young age. An initiate (use the **cultist** stat block) trains for months or years before gaining any rank within the organization, and many trainees don't survive the tests. An initiate who passes the tests must choose an affinity to a particular color of dragon: black, blue, green, red, or white. He or she is then welcomed into the ranks as a dragonclaw.

The higher ranks of the cult, in ascending order, are dragonclaw, dragonwing, dragonfang, dragonsoul, and wyrmspeaker. There are only five wyrmspeakers, one per color of chromatic dragon. The current wyrmspeakers are Severin (red), Galvan (blue), Neronvain (green), Rezmir (black), and Varram (white).

Most of the cult's operations are overseen by local leaders called Wearers of Purple for the ceremonial robes that they wear. All of the wyrmspeakers are Wearers of Purple, as are lower-ranking cultists appointed by the wyrmspeakers to preside over cult enclaves.

The trail leads south about twelve miles, to a more rugged region where steep-sided, rocky plateaus replace the gently rolling hills. The land between the plateaus is largely flat, broken only by outcroppings and wandering streams in steep-sided gullies. The plateaus jut fifty to one hundred feet above their surroundings and are difficult to climb except where rock falls and subsidence created natural ramps. The crumbling sides of the plateaus are dotted with caves and tumbled boulder fields.

Characters can have two encounters during this trip. The first is with a group of raiders who have straggled behind the main body. They are disorganized and quarrelsome, and they should be easy prey for alert adventurers. The second group is an organized rearguard watching specifically for pursuers from the town. They present a much graver threat.

Stragglers

Characters spot this group's cooking fire smoke from several miles away, because the stragglers stopped to roast a few prairie hens for a meal. They sought shelter in a low spot between surrounding hills, where tall boulders have rolled into a loose jumble. In fact, the surroundings offer no protection while making it easier for enemies to sneak up on the site.

By observing for a few minutes, characters can discern that there are four human **cultists** and eight **kobolds** in the group. The kobolds and humans distrust each other, and although the cultists act as if they're the bosses, their leadership amounts to nothing more than ineffectual bullying. The humans' weapons are stacked against a rock, out of easy reach. The kobolds have their weapons on their belts.

If the group is left alone, the kobolds grab their share of the half-cooked lunch and move about fifty yards away to eat, while the humans continue squabbling over how to cook a hen and the uselessness of kobolds as allies.

If characters choose to bypass this group, a detour can get them around it with no difficulty. They could run into these stragglers again on their way back to Greenest.

If characters attack, then unless they give away their presence on purpose (by hailing the camp, for example), they gain a surprise round. The humans spend their first turns retrieving their weapons and shields. The kobolds drop their food and scatter, then regroup and counterattack on round four, using their slings as much as possible. They stick around and fight only as long as any of their human allies are still fighting. As soon as the humans are all defeated, the remaining kobolds slink away into the hills and aren't seen again.

Rewards. Award standard XP for defeated foes, including kobolds that ran away. If any cultists are questioned, they refuse to talk unless someone succeeds at a DC 15 Charisma (Intimidation) check. They know it's standard practice for a raiding party to leave behind a rearguard. They don't know how strong the rearguard will be, but they expect it is sited about a mile ahead where the path passes between rocky bluffs. They also can describe the raiders' camp and its location, plus they know some prisoners were taken from the town but not how many or whether they include a half-elf monk. They know the raid was for loot, because they were told to look specifically for gold, gems, and other valuables and were forbidden to do any looting for themselves. Cultists know they are preparing "the great hoard to honor the Dragon Queen."

Captured kobolds talk freely, but most of what they say is lies. That's not because they try to mislead enemies, but because they will say anything, no matter how outlandish, if it might gain them their freedom.

The cultists have 28 sp among them, besides their cheap weapons. The kobolds, who looted despite their orders, have a sack containing pewter candlesticks, some silver serving dishes, and a few religious carvings of Chauntea taken from a home shrine.

REARGUARD

If the characters learn of the camp location and probable site of the rearguard from the stragglers, they can use that information to bypass this encounter entirely. In fact, that would be the smart thing to do, both because it negates a damaging fight and because if the rearguard is wiped out, leaders in the cult will wonder why it never reported back. The best result for the characters is if the outpost checks in at the correct time with an "all clear."

The rearguard consists of one **veteran**, six **cultists**, and two **acolytes**. The guard and cultists have spears for both ranged and melee combat. They are positioned in an area where the trail winds through a gap between two outcrops. The ambushers are hidden in the rocks, 12 to 15 feet above ground level. Characters might detect the ambush, with the odds depending on what they know and how they approach the area.

- If stragglers described the likely ambush spot to characters, it can be recognized from 200 yards away with a successful DC 10 Wisdom (Perception) check.
- If stragglers mentioned the rearguard but didn't describe the spot, it is recognized as a good spot for an ambush from 100 yards away with a successful DC 15 Wisdom (Perception) check.
- If characters haven't been warned about the rearguard, someone spots a face peering down from above with a successful DC 20 Wisdom (Perception)

check, but not until the characters are within 20 yards.

- If players state that they're watching for potential ambush spots, give them advantage when making these checks.

The rearguard has a twofold mission. It must stop any small party of intruders coming up the trail, or harass and delay a larger group while sending word to the camp that trouble approaches. The veteran decides that he has enough of an advantage against a party of five or six adventurers to deal with the problem on the spot, provided he doesn't weaken his force by sending a runner to Frulam Mondath. If the adventuring group contains seven or more characters, you can either have the veteran harass the enemy and dispatch a runner to the camp, or you can add cultists until they outnumber the characters by two or three, then let the cultists make a stand.

If characters walk into the trap, the cultists tumble boulders onto them. Each character must succeed on a DC 11 Dexterity saving throw or take 2d12 bludgeoning damage from falling rocks (half as much damage on a successful save). The boulder attack constitutes the cultists' surprise round. After that, they use ranged attacks until they are out of ammunition or the heroes force them into melee. Because they are positioned in the rocks above the characters, the cultists have three-quarters cover against attacks from below (+5 bonus to AC). To reach the foes, characters must scramble up the rocks. The distance is only 10 to 15 feet and no ability check is required, but the rocks are difficult terrain.

DEVELOPMENTS

These raiders are distinctly different from the earlier stragglers. All are dressed in similar (but not identical) black leather tunics with flared, black mantles. These are dedicated cultists. If captured, nothing less than a successful DC 20 Charisma (Intimidation) check can pry any information from them. Even with that, all they reveal is that they are initiates in the Cult of the Dragon, the names of their leaders (Rezmir, Frulam Mondath, and Langdedrosa Cyanwrath), and that the raid on Greenest was to collect treasure for dragons. Rezmir outranks the other leaders.

FRULAM MONDATH

RAIDER CAMP

LEVEL 3

LEVEL 1

LEVEL 2

2

4

3

~OVERVIEW~

100FT 200FT 300FT

BLANDO

Rewards. Award standard XP for defeated foes. The cultists have no treasure, but their Cult of the Dragon outfits and weapons could be invaluable when characters try to get into the raiders' camp.

THE CAMP

The cultists have set up their camp in the hollow of a rocky plateau that's shaped roughly like a horseshoe. The lower portion of the plateau rises gently from the surrounding land, but it quickly steepens and ascends to a height of 150 feet above the landscape. Boulders form jumbled heaps at the bases of the cliffs. The level shelves and top of the plateau are covered in long grass, and brush and scrubby trees grow in patches.

GENERAL FEATURES

Boulders. The boulders are difficult terrain and provide three-quarters cover.

Brush. The brush around the site grows to a height of 4 to 6 feet. It is tough and dense, making it difficult terrain and providing three-quarters cover to targets sheltering among it.

Caves. The steep sides of the plateau are dotted with shallow caves. Boulders or brush conveniently conceals many of the cave mouths. Characters who need to take a long rest can easily find a secure cave in which to hide.

Guard Towers. The cultists have built two guard towers at the camp, one at the entrance to the hollow

and one atop the plateau. These towers are 20 feet high and made from rough timbers lashed together with rope. They are large enough for a few lookouts. The tower at the mouth of the hollow is manned by kobolds, while warriors man the one above. The guards have horns to blow when they must sound an alarm.

Prisoners. The cultists' prisoners are kept at area 1. Currently, only eight prisoners are in the camp, not counting Leosin. During the day, they are put to work under guard by four **dragonclaws** (see appendix B). At night, they are shackled to a post in their hut to prevent escape. The shackles are secured by a single chain and lock that can be opened with a key carried by one of the guards or with thieves' tools and a successful DC 10 Dexterity check. The chain can be broken with a successful DC 20 Strength check. Five of the prisoners are from Greenest, and the other three are from earlier raids against hamlets and small farming villages to the south and east. There were more prisoners at one time, but many have died from overwork and mistreatment. If a situation develops where released prisoners must fight, use **commoner** stats for them.

Slopes. The sides of the plateau rise sharply, while the floor of the hollow slopes up gradually toward the east. A long ladder is lashed to the cliff so guards can reach the upper guard tower.

The cliffs have handholds and footholds for climbing, so no die roll is needed under normal circumstances. If characters are in a hurry, a successful DC 10 Strength

(Athletics) check is needed to make the climb without falling. If characters are concerned about keeping quiet, then a successful DC 10 Dexterity (Stealth) check ensures that no rocks break loose and rattle down.

Tents. The raiders live in circular huts made from closely spaced wooden or bone poles covered in hide, mud, and sod. Huts vary in diameter from 10 feet to 25 feet, and in height from 5 feet to 10 feet. (Symbols on the map represent clusters of tents.) Those in the mouth of the hollow (level 1 on the map) are crudely built and decorated with animal skulls. These are occupied by kobolds. Cultists occupy the huts on level 2, which are sturdier, cleaner, and decorated with painted designs representing dragons. A few tents on level 2 are set aside for prisoners.

The large tent at area 2 is set apart from the others by an open space. It is reserved for Rezmir, Frulam Mondath, Langdedrosa Cyanwrath, and Azbara Jos. An honor guard of four **veterans** and four **guard drakes** (appendix B) keeps watch around this tent day and night. They don't sleep at their posts, they don't fall for tricks, and they don't listen to stories or pleas. Their job is to keep everyone away from the tent, and they are fanatical about it. Only acolytes and adepts the veterans know by sight and by voice are allowed to approach.

Camp Alertness

For the first day following the raid, the cultists are both elated with the outcome and exhausted. Rezmir doesn't expect a serious challenge from the town, and slower members of the raiding party and walking wounded straggle into camp all through the day after the raid. The situation at the camp is confused and security is lax. Most of these raiders are mercenaries and bandits, and not even the dedicated cultists wear recognizable uniforms on raids. No one challenges latecomers for passwords or security signals. Put simply, the raiders are confident that no enemies followed them this far. Characters can walk straight into the camp without having their identities seriously challenged. In fact, the bolder they are, the more likely they are to blend right in.

Players may be tempted to have characters seek cover and observe during the day and not attempt to enter the camp until nightfall. This can work, too, but sneaking around in the dark is more likely to attract suspicion than simply walking in as if they belong in the camp.

The chief risk is that someone might recognize the characters from the fighting at Greenest. Have each character make a DC 5 Charisma check. Success means no one remembers the character's face, but failure means that at some time (not necessarily immediately, but when recognition would be the most dramatic), someone in the camp recognizes the character. If characters are wearing Cult of the Dragon regalia taken from the rearguard, the characters have disadvantage on this roll because no one returning to camp at this time should be in uniform. The character who faced Cyanwrath one-on-one, however, has a -4 penalty to the roll. If that character ever comes face-to-face with

the half-dragon, recognition is automatic.

As the day wears on and the commotion winds down, the camp becomes calmer and better organized. Guards resume their normal routines. If characters haven't entered the camp before sundown of the first day, they find it more difficult, since there's very little traffic in and out of the camp on a normal day. They'll need a good story and a successful DC 10 Charisma (Deception) check to walk past a guard station of five **guards**. This check can be made only once for the group; they can't talk their way out of a failure. After the initial opportunity to enter the camp has passed, characters need to resort to stealth or subterfuge to get in. For example, characters scaling the plateau from the east could use brush for cover right up to where the cliff overlooks the camp. From there, they could observe or climb down the rocks under cover of darkness.

The whole camp goes on alert if the bodies of murdered human sentries or cultists are discovered. One dead kobold won't cause much alarm, but many dead kobolds will. If the camp goes on alert, every character must make a DC 15 Charisma check. A failure means the character has been spotted as a stranger and an infiltrator. Someone raises the hue and cry, which quickly draws a crowd. A roll of 10 or lower means

LANGDEDROSA CYANWRATH

BRYAN SYME

someone has recognized the character from the fight in Greenest. The characters have a chance to get away if they immediately go on the attack and begin cutting their way out of camp, but if they delay or spin tales, a crowd of **cultists** that outnumbers them five to one surrounds them.

If characters try to estimate numbers in the camp, they count roughly one hundred kobolds and a mix of bandits, guards, and cultists totaling about eighty—effectively an unlimited supply if characters get the idea of fighting them all.

Captured!

If caught, characters are disarmed, their hands are tied, and they are brought before Frulam Mondath for judgment. One by one, she asks them who they are, where they came from, and what they're doing in her camp.

- If anyone was recognized from the fighting in Greenest, it doesn't matter what the characters say. Mondath sentences all of them to be executed on the morrow, after spending the night tied to posts alongside the monk Leosin. Characters have one night to escape this fate. They might wriggle out of their bonds, bribe or charm a cultist to set them free, or come up with a clever use for a cantrip. If all else fails, Leosin reveals that he has a hidden knife with which they can cut themselves free.
- If characters admit they came from Greenest and are enemies of the cult, the effect is the same as if they'd been recognized.
- If characters lie to Mondath—claiming they are new recruits and this is all a mistake, for example, or that they are studying the cult before deciding whether to join—then compare their Charisma (Deception) checks to Mondath's Wisdom check to determine whether she believes them. You can allow advantage or disadvantage on the roll when someone's lies are especially plausible or implausible. Match die rolls individually for every character. Those who Mondath believes are set free, but watched and stopped if they try to leave the camp. Those who Mondath does not believe are sentenced to die as above.

Exploring the Camp

Characters can learn much from poking around in the camp. If the characters pose as cult members, they can speak to other cultists and question them (carefully) about the cult's plans and long-term goals. Most cultists should be treated as indifferent when determining reactions or trying to gain a favor. Kobolds are less helpful and should be considered hostile when characters make Charisma checks to gauge their reaction.

Characters can learn the following information through observation and questioning. They need to be careful, however, not to attract attention for asking too many questions or poking their noses into things that are none of their business. Any time they come off as "too nosy," feel free to call for another Charisma check to see whether someone recognizes them from Greenest.

- This is a camp of the Cult of the Dragon—praise Tiamat's glory! (Some cultists extend their right hand with fingers outstretched to represent the five heads of Tiamat when they praise her glory. Others curl back two fingers, to show that Tiamat's strength is hidden. This is not mandatory, but adepts and hard-core cultists look favorably on those who do it sincerely.)
- Not everyone here is a full-fledged member of the cult. Many are new initiates working toward full acceptance, and many others are simple mercenaries, hired to flesh out the camp's strength during raids or if it should come under attack.
- The kobolds are here because their worshipful attitude toward dragons makes them easy for Rezmir and other high-ranking cultists to manipulate, but they are not well liked or trusted by the other races.
- Hunters who bring in antelope and other large game from the grasslands feed the camp. The cultists and their allies eat most of it, but some is stored in the cave to feed the hatchlings.
- The cult has been ranging far and wide on small raids to collect treasure. Greenest was the closest target to the camp, the biggest of all the towns they've attacked, and the most profitable—praise Tiamat's glory!
- Prisoners are used for manual labor. In the past, a few have "converted" and become loyal members of the cult, but most die eventually of overwork and undernourishment. Then they are fed to the drakes or taken into the cave to feed the hatchlings.
- The cave at the back of the camp (area 4) is off-limits to all but those who've been cleared by Mondath and Rezmir, which includes a handful of guards and kobolds. It's known around camp as "the nursery," and it's an open secret that Rezmir plans to hatch a clutch of dragon eggs there.
- The half-black dragon Rezmir came to the area a few months ago, and she set up the camp. Mondath handles everyday operations.
- The half-blue dragon Cyanwrath is Mondath's right hand and is seldom far from her side. He has a rigid sense of honor, but you don't want to make him angry.
- The mother of dragons—praise Tiamat's glory—shall return, and when that day comes, all the nations of the world shall tremble before her majesty!
- The monk is of special interest to Rezmir. Why else would she keep the creature alive that way? What Rezmir hopes to learn from him is anyone's guess, but you wouldn't want to be in that half-elf's skin—or what's left of it—when the questioning gets serious.
- The plunder from nearby settlements is stored in the cave. No one but Rezmir knows how much is there altogether, but it must be a big pile by now.

Aside from being recognized, the chief risk of spending time in the cultist camp is getting roped into a work detail. Characters might be selected by an officer to spend a few hours helping with food preparation, standing guard in a tower, practicing weapon drill, or even cleaning up after animals (a job usually reserved for prisoners, but currently the number of prisoners in the camp is low).

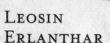

LEOSIN ERLANTHAR

The monk is tied to a stake at the back of the camp (area 3). He has been severely beaten, and he has been denied food and water in an effort to break his spirit. Rezmir knows from informants across the Sword Coast that Leosin has been researching the cult's history and recent activity. The wyrmspeaker wants to know how much Leosin has learned and with whom he shared his information. Rezmir considered it an amazing stroke of luck that Leosin was captured during the raid.

In fact, it wasn't luck at all, at least not for Rezmir. Leosin had studied their previous attacks and concluded that the time was right for the cult to strike a bigger target, and he knew that Greenest was prosperous yet poorly defended, making it the most likely next target. So, when he deemed the time was just about right, he visited the town with the intent of staying until something happened. His observations paid off, and Leosin separated from his people during the night and fell in with the raiders when they retreated, hoping to learn more about the cult's plans and the location of their camp. Rezmir spotted him after the sun came up, and the monk was quickly overpowered and captured.

That portion of Leosin's scheme has worked reasonably well. He now knows most of the information listed above under "Exploring the Camp." Unfortunately for him, captivity has been more brutal than he expected, and although his mind and will are still strong, he's in a very poor physical state.

Despite the danger, Leosin isn't entirely happy about being rescued if characters come to set him free. He believes he can learn more, and he's willing to take the risk. He's too weak to resist, however, so characters can easily take him away against his will if that's what they want to do. He can move without aid at a speed of 20 feet and fights as a commoner with disadvantage on attack rolls. If characters don't bring him out of the camp, Leosin breaks away on his own. He refuses to talk about it later.

If characters are captured and imprisoned alongside Leosin and their attempts to escape fall through, he reveals that he has a small knife hidden in his boot. They can use it to cut their bonds. Leosin's absence is noticed within five minutes if he is taken away, and an alarm goes up throughout the camp. Rigging up a dummy in his place delays the discovery by twenty minutes. Tying up a dead or unconscious cultist (preferably a half-elf) in his place assures the intruders a two-hour head start before the escape is noticed.

REWARDS

Award standard XP for defeated foes. This episode does not involve many fights, but it does present many challenges, and characters should be rewarded for overcoming them. The awards listed below are just recommendations; adjust them and add to them as you see fit. Characters can reach 3rd level if they act prudently and capitalize on all the opportunities the camp offers, but it's not essential that they do.

- If you are using the milestone experience rule, the characters reach 3rd level when they complete this episode.
- For getting into and out of the cultists' camp without causing an alarm or being caught: 100 XP per character.
- For getting into and out of the cultists' camp without stirring any suspicion: an additional 100 XP per character.
- For rescuing Leosin: 250 XP per character.
- For leaving a dummy or decoy in Leosin's place: an additional 50 XP per character.
- For rescuing other prisoners: 25 XP for each prisoner brought out of the camp alive.
- For each piece of information listed under "Exploring the Camp" that characters learn on their own (not from Leosin): 25 XP per character.

When the characters arrive safely back at Greenest—presumably with Leosin in tow—he can fill them in on any details they missed during their investigation of the cult's camp. The monks who accompanied him are delighted to see him alive, and the families of any other released prisoners are equally grateful for the return of their loved ones. Governor Nighthill pays the characters their promised 250 gp each and publicly praises their courage and daring.

EPISODE 3: DRAGON HATCHERY

After his experience in captivity, Leosin needs several days to recover. When he's healthy again, he intends to travel north to Elturel to convey what he's learned to Ontharr Frume, a paladin of Torm who shares his concern over the Cult of the Dragon's recent surge in activity. He has a favor to ask of the characters.

> "After all you've done already for me personally and for the people of Greenest, I hate to ask anything more from you. But the need is great, and I dare to hope that you can aid me one time more. I need you to return to the cultists' camp. You know your way around it now. If the cultists are preparing to conduct another raid, or a large body of them marches away, or if anything substantial is carried into or out of that cave, I need to know. If you have a chance to get into the camp and look around again, that would be the ideal way to spot anything that's changed.
>
> "I don't recommend letting yourselves get captured," he adds with a wry smile.

If the characters were working as caravan guards, Leosin offers to match whatever their previous employer was paying them plus 20 percent. If they are currently unemployed, he offers them 150 gp apiece. He's willing to haggle; this mission is important, and no one else is available who Leosin believes can handle it. If the characters accept, he tells them to find him at the city of Elturel afterward, both to report and to collect their pay. If he has moved on before they reach the city, they can speak to the paladin Ontharr Frume instead.

The monk doesn't believe it's essential that the characters head back to the camp immediately. He doesn't expect the cultists to make any sudden changes in their plans or mode of operation. Leosin is wrong about this, because he doesn't realize how much his presence in Greenest alarmed the wyrmspeaker. Rezmir knows that Leosin is investigating the Cult of the Dragon, but she doesn't know whether the monk's appearance in Greenest was a coincidence, a good guess, or a sign that the cult's whole plan has been compromised. She isn't willing to take chances: she's heading north with the accumulated treasure immediately.

Abandoned Camp

When characters return to the camp area, they find it mostly abandoned. (If they stayed, they witnessed the rapid packing up and abandonment of the camp.) The stinking huts of the kobolds (those on level 1) have been burned, but the level 2 huts and both guard towers remain. Anyone can determine from tracks that the cultists trekked away in small groups in all directions. A successful DC 10 Wisdom (Perception) check reveals that most of the camp's wagons and pack animals moved in a train toward the west.

Still left in the camp are some hunters, the kobolds who tend the dragon nursery in the caves, Frulam Mondath, her guards, and Langdedrosa Cyanwrath. Only the hunters still use the huts. All others live in the hatchery cave. The activity and guards around the cave mouth should be the top draw on the characters' attention.

On most mornings, hunters fan out onto the grassland to hunt for antelope and other large game. They travel on horseback and bring along an extra horse to pack the field-dressed game back to the camp. Hunters don't necessarily return to the camp every evening. They stay out until they have a load of meat to bring back. Hunting on the Greenfields is good, so they seldom need to spend more than a night or two away. Four **scouts** act as hunters; roll a d4 to determine how many are in the camp when characters arrive. They are not dedicated cultists, so they won't challenge characters who enter the camp, attack them, or even alert the cultists. They consider standing guard to be beneath them.

They are a taciturn bunch, so they won't be much help to inquisitive characters. They converse more freely with rangers, but to most strangers they merely nod, point, shake their heads, scowl, and utter one- or two-word answers. If characters converse with them, these hunters can relate how the camp dissolved within hours after the discovery of the captured half-elf's escape. Crates carried from the cave were loaded onto wagons or animals and hauled to the west. A few raiders remain in the cave: the Wearer of Purple (Mondath), the "dragon-man" (Cyanwrath), the better warriors, and the "dragon-dogs" (kobolds). As long as the cultists pay well for fresh meat, the trackers continue hunting for them. Whatever else the cave holds is none of their concern.

A thorough search of the camp takes about ten man-hours. Allow characters to make a Wisdom (Perception) check after the first hour. A successful roll means the character realizes that while quite a bit of material has been left behind, it's all trash: cracked pottery, rusty knives, soiled clothing and bedding, cheap cookware, and wine that's gone to vinegar. Some of it might be of use to the people of Greenest who lost everything in fires, but it has no value as treasure.

General Features

The only thing of interest remaining in the camp is the cave itself (area 4 on the map of the camp), which characters can see from the camp. There, characters find the cultists who stayed behind, a clutch of dragon eggs, the special cadre of kobolds who tend the eggs—and the many traps the kobolds set to defend their home. These eggs are important to the cult, but they were deemed too near to hatching to be moved safely. Rezmir left them with what he believed was an adequate guard force under Frulam Mondath and Langdedrosa Cyanwrath.

Ceilings. Cavern ceilings are 15 feet high. Ceilings in the humans' chambers (areas 11, 12, and 13) are 10 feet high.

Light. During daytime, areas 1 and 2 are brightly lit, and areas 3 and 4 are dimly lit by outside light. All other areas are in darkness unless the area notes otherwise.

Sound. The caverns are filled with faint sounds: dripping water, scratching rodents, scrabbling lizards, wind moaning across the entrance. These normal underground sounds camouflage the clanks, thuds, coughs, and speech of the kobolds and cultists. Sound echoes well along the main chamber (areas 1–5), so a fight in any of these can be heard in the others. Elsewhere, normal sounds echo confusingly and are lost in the background noise. The sound of a scream carries a long distance, however, and the sound of a fight travels through 30 feet of tunnel and attracts attention if the fight lasts more than 3 rounds.

Wandering Monsters

Kobolds move freely through the caverns, going about their business. Characters have a chance to randomly encounter these wandering kobolds. Roll a d6 every time characters enter or re-enter areas 3 to 10. On a roll of 1, monsters are present. Roll on the table to determine what they meet. These randomly encountered monsters are added to any creatures mentioned in the area description. Be sure to make this roll before characters enter the area, because both groups have a chance to gain surprise.

Episode 3 Encounters

d6	Encounter
1	4 kobolds
2	6 kobolds, 2 winged kobolds
3	3 winged kobolds
4	5 winged kobolds
5	2 winged kobolds, 1 guard drake (appendix B)
6	2 ambush drakes (appendix B)

1. Cave Entrance

The entrance to the cave is broad and tall, but the ceiling quickly lowers to a height of 15 feet. Standing guard inside the entrance are two **dragonclaws** (see appendix B). They position themselves about 30 feet inside the cave and stay near the walls and the column, so that while they aren't hidden, they aren't conspicuous, either. Characters who observe the cave from a distance—from the area of the plateau where the steps ascend from level 1 to level 2, for example—spot one of the dragonclaws.

If characters approach openly through the camp, the dragonclaws spot them automatically and retreat toward area 2 in the cave, to set up an ambush. If characters approach the cave quietly from the sides, they won't be spotted. They then have a chance to surprise the dragonclaws.

2. Concealed Passage

If the guards at the entrance spotted the characters' approach, they wait here until the characters come into view, then try to spring an ambush. Determine surprise normally.

The passage at the end of this alcove is deeply shadowed and hidden by a cleverly cut fold in the rock. It's obvious to anyone who walks to the end of the alcove, but from elsewhere in the cavern, it can be spotted only with a successful DC 20 Wisdom (Perception) check.

The stairs down to area 3 are trapped. See that area's description for details.

3. Fungus Garden

The kobolds cultivate fungus in this cavern to supplement the meat brought in by the hunters. Mixed in among the mundane fungi are violet fungi. The drop-off from area 2 is 10 feet high. The stairs are trapped; see below.

> The entrance to the cave ends here at a 10-foot drop-off. To your right, broad steps are roughly hewn into a natural stone ramp. The cavern below is carpeted with a profusion of fungi ranging from a few inches high to nearly as tall as a human adult. Two paths lead through the fungi: one on the right and one on the left.

Nothing distinguishes the paths to casual inspection. The path on the right is flanked by four **violet fungi**, while the path on the left is free of these dangerous growths. The violet fungi can be spotted among all the other mushrooms with a successful DC 15 Intelligence (Nature) check, but only from the base of the steps, not from atop the ledge. Likewise, a careful inspection of the path reveals that only the left trail sees heavy use.

Trapped Stairs

The stairs are constructed so that the lowest steps collapse into a ramp that dumps a character right at the base of the violet fungi. Roll any die as each character descends the steps; on an odd roll, the character triggers the trap. A character who is actively looking for a trap on the stairs can find the trapped step with a successful DC 15 Wisdom (Perception) check. The kobolds and guards know where to avoid stepping, of course.

4. Stirge Lair

Some fungus from area 3 dots this area, but chiefly it is the lair of a colony of bats. Hidden among the bats are ten **stirges**. The bats are present only from sunrise to sundown, but the stirges are always here. Normally the stirges prey on the plentiful bats and leave the cave's other residents alone, but not always.

Characters notice dead bats on the floor (victims of the stirges). If that causes someone to look up, describe how the ceiling is carpeted with bats with a successful DC 10 Wisdom (Perception) check. To avoid startling the bats, characters must proceed very quietly. This requires a successful DC 10 Dexterity (Stealth) check. If three or more characters fail the check, the bats are alarmed by the noise, drop from the ceiling, and fly through the cavern in a blinding cloud of flapping and squeaking rodents. The bats present no danger, but their racket drowns out other noise and makes it impossible to see more than 5 feet. It also alerts the stirges, and the opportunistic bloodsuckers attack in the confusion. The stirges gain a +2 bonus to AC in the bat storm.

The bats calm down and return to their roosts on the ceiling after five minutes of quiet in area 4.

A spear with a pitted blade lies on the floor near the top of the steps leading to area 6. Kobolds use this to bypass the trap at the bottom of the steps (see area 6).

5. Troglodyte Incursion

The floor drops down 10 feet at each ledge.

Kobolds use this portion of the cave as a trash dump. Along with normal sorts of refuse, such as broken pottery, rotted baskets, and mouse-chewed rope, they've also thrown out items that appear useful from a distance: discarded clothes, worn boots, tattered books, cracked lamps, and so forth. Some of these items came from prisoners who died, and others were taken in treasure raids and later deemed to be unworthy of Tiamat. Characters viewing this area from the ledge see tantalizing glints of metal (belt buckles without belts) and parchment (books rendered illegible by water damage).

A strong, foul smell hangs in the air. Troglodytes that live deeper beneath the ground have made incursions into the cave through narrow crevices (not displayed on the map). If characters give this area a cursory look and then leave, nothing happens here. If they spend time searching, then four **troglodytes** attack. The crevices are a potential area for characters to explore if you'd like to expand this dungeon for further adventures. If not, then declare that they're too tight for characters to squeeze through, or eliminate them and the troglodytes entirely.

Treasure

A thorough search of the trash heap, taking 10 minutes, does find one worthwhile item: an overlooked pouch of six ornamental gems worth 10 gp each and eight semi-precious gems worth 50 gp each. The troglodytes have nothing that anyone would want near them.

6. Meat Locker

The curtain across the entrance to this cavern is trapped. See "Trapped Curtain" below for details.

> At the base of these steeply descending steps, a curtain hangs across the passage. It is made from hundreds of heavy leather strips, each about the width of a human hand. The strips are fixed to the ceiling and are long enough to drag on the floor. The curtain extends from wall to wall. The leather comes from a variety of local animals and is badly cured. The curtain is several layers thick with no gaps, so you can't see through it at all.

This cavern is naturally cold. It hovers a few degrees above freezing year round, regardless of the season.

Much of the meat brought in by the hunters feeds the cultists and the kobolds, but the extra is stored here for eventual use when the dragon eggs hatch and the ravenous hatchlings emerge. The carcasses range from very fresh to several months old. The meat is only cold, not frozen, so the older items are slowly going bad.

> The smell of old blood assaults your nose. The floor is covered with dried puddles of it. Four floor-to-ceiling columns are spaced across the chamber, and chains have been strung between them like clothesline. Animal carcasses hang on hooks from the chains. You see gutted and skinned antelope, deer, goats, what might be big cats, and even a few small bears. Some of this meat has been here for a while if the smell is a reliable indicator.

This cave contains nothing of value.

TRAPPED CURTAIN
Hidden in the patches of fur still clinging to the leather strips of the curtain are hundreds of metal barbs about the size of large fishhooks. The barbs are coated with poison. Anyone who brushes through the curtain must succeed on a DC 10 Dexterity saving throw or take 5 (1d10) poison damage, and the target's hit point maximum is reduced by 5. This reduction lasts until the target finishes a long rest.

A careful inspection of the leather strips coupled with a successful DC 10 Wisdom (Perception) check finds barbs; they can't be noticed otherwise. When kobolds use this stairway, they bring the ruined spear that's kept in area 4. With it, they sweep the leather strips to the left side of the corridor and wedge the end of the spear shaft into an angled socket in the floor just inside area 6. This holds the leather strips safely out of the way while they move in and out of the chamber.

7. DRAKE NURSERY
The short, wide passage between areas 4 and 7 is trapped. See "Spike Trap" below for details. Simple oil lamps provide dim, flickering light. This chamber contains four **kobolds** and one **winged kobold**. These creatures are in the upper part of the chamber.

The lower area is where cultists conducted the rituals to create their guard drakes and then housed the creatures. The ledge is a sharp 10-foot drop-off. Wooden stairs descend at the right end of the ledge. A stout cage made of iron bars surrounds these steps to a height of 10 feet to prevent untrained drakes from escaping up the steps. A key hangs on a peg at the top of the steps; it opens the locked gate at the bottom.

A rack along the southwest wall holds implements used in training the drakes: long poles with lassos at the end, used for snaring and controlling young drakes; leashes and collars; sharp prods; mock weapons made

of wood; human-sized dummies stitched out of sailcloth and stuffed with straw, with ridiculous expressions painted on their faces.

The lower area is heavily shadowed. Currently it holds three **guard drakes** that are near the end of their training. Being not quite fully developed, they have the normal stats of a guard drake but only 33 hit points. Spotting these drakes from the ledge requires a successful DC 15 Wisdom (Perception) check; sweeping the pit with a bullseye lantern grants advantage on this check. If characters bring some raw meat to the ledge, the drakes think they're about to be fed and advance into the light. If characters enter the pit, either by descending the steps or climbing down the ledge, the drakes attack.

If the drakes are spotted and attacked by characters on the ledge, they set up a howl that draws six **kobolds** and three **winged kobolds** from area 8. At least one of these try to get past the characters and unlock the gate at the bottom of the steps, letting the guard drakes join the battle as they've been trained to do.

Spike Trap

A portion of the floor between areas 4 and 7 has been replaced with a sheet of parchment cleverly painted to resemble the surrounding stone. It can be spotted with a successful DC 15 Wisdom (Perception) check, or automatically by someone who is systematically tapping the floor ahead with a pole or other tool. Beneath the parchment sheet is a shallow pit (about 2 feet deep) lined with poisoned spikes. Each time a character moves between areas 4 and 7, roll a d10. On a roll of 1 or 2, that character's foot has gone through the trap. The character takes 1d4 piercing damage from the spikes and must make a DC 10 Constitution saving throw against poison. On a failed save, the character is affected as by a *confusion* spell for one minute (10 rounds). On a successful save, the character is affected as by a *confusion* spell for 1 round. The effect is not magical.

8. Kobold Barracks

The steps down from area 7 are trapped; see "Collapsing Trap" below for details. Area 8 is the kobolds' living quarters. It was a natural cavern, but it has been enlarged and smoothed in a crude manner. Unless they already responded to noise in area 7, this area contains six **kobolds** and six **winged kobolds**. They are off duty, so they aren't being especially alert. Use their passive Wisdom (Perception) scores to determine whether they react to noises. Flickering oil lamps provide dim illumination.

> Thin mattresses of straw covered with badly cured furs form small beds that are haphazardly positioned around the chamber. Rats and small lizards scurry through the food scraps and moldy wine skins littering the floor.

A search of the room takes 10 minutes and turns up 38 gp, 152 sp, and 704 cp sorted into eighty-eight stacks of exactly eight copper coins each. Dozens of dragon-themed talismans and amulets are carved from bone, soapstone, wood, and ivory. The workmanship on most

of them is terrible, but four have a unique, if savage, artistic flair. These are worth 50, 60, 70, and 100 gp respectively if sold to a collector of artistic oddities. To any other merchant, they are worth 10 gp each.

Collapsing Trap

The top step is rigged to drop a portion of the ceiling in area 7. As each character enters the staircase, roll any die. On an odd roll, the character steps in the wrong spot and triggers the trap. The ceiling collapses above the next character in line (the one behind the character who triggered the trap). That character takes 4d4 bludgeoning damage from falling rocks; the damage is halved if the character makes a successful DC 15 Dexterity saving throw. Every character within 5 feet takes 2d4 bludgeoning damage, or half that with a successful saving throw.

A character who is actively looking for a trap on the stairs can find the trapped step with a successful DC 10 Wisdom (Perception) check. The collapsible ceiling is spotted incidentally with a successful DC 15 Wisdom (Perception) check.

The kobolds in areas 8 and 9 hear the commotion if the trap is set off.

9. Dragon Shrine

This cave is a shrine to Tiamat, but with an emphasis on her black dragon head and on black dragons in general. It also contains many Cult of the Dragon icons, and a devious trap for the unwary; see "Acid Trap" below. Flickering oil lamps provide dim light.

Langdedrosa Cyanwrath occupies the shrine, and he is joined by two human **berserkers**. (If the adventuring party contains more than four characters, add one more berserker for each additional character. If Langdedrosa was killed, then replace him with another half-dragon with the same statistics.) If Cyanwrath fought any of the characters one-on-one in Greenest, he immediately singles out that person to address as follows.

> "You survived! I don't know whether to be disappointed or pleased. It's a mix of both, I think."

If the character beat the odds in Greenest and won the fight, you can paraphrase to reflect that. As soon as he finishes speaking, he attacks. As long as none of the characters intervene, Cyanwrath's group knows better than to interfere in his one-on-one matches. If the characters gang up on Cyanwrath or one of his guards, or try to leave the chamber, the guards attack.

If none of the characters fought Cyanwrath during the raid but spent time in the cultists' camp, read this.

> "You look familiar . . . I've seen you around the camp. If you came looking for trouble, I am the trouble you seek."

Then he attacks, and his guards join in immediately.

The creatures in area 10 are not drawn to this fight. They hide and wait to see who wins. When the fight is over, characters have time to investigate the room.

This chamber has been enlarged and reshaped from its original form. The floor and three of the walls are smooth, and stalactites and stalagmites have been polished into gleaming columns. Every surface glistens with moisture, and the air is warm and humid. The flat walls of the chamber are decorated with shallow abstract carvings of dragons. Dragons' tails coil into intricate patterns and knots that flow across the walls. The creature portrayed in the northwest corner stands out: a five-headed dragon, rising from an erupting volcano. Other dragons, which seem dwarfed by the five-headed monstrosity, flock to its side. A small, wooden chest with silver and mother-of-pearl inlays sits on the floor in the corner, in front of the monstrous dragon carving.

The five-headed dragon is Tiamat, and the volcano is the Well of Dragons, where the Cult of the Dragon intends to bring Tiamat into the world. The Well of Dragons is located at the northern extreme of the Sunset Mountains. Most characters should recognize Tiamat from folktales and know she was banished to the Nine Hells long ago and remains imprisoned there. There is no way to tell from the carvings where the volcano is located, or to know if it's meant to be a prediction of events to come or just a birth metaphor for the queen of evil dragons.

The chest is locked and trapped; see "Acid Trap" below for details. Characters can open it with the key from area 11, or the lock can be picked with thieves' tools and a successful DC 10 Dexterity check. Unless the Dexterity roll is 15 or higher, however, it sets off the trap when the chest opens.

If characters spend 10 minutes or more studying the carvings, they can learn two things. First, black dragons are overrepresented. Almost half the dragons shown appear to be black dragons. Wyrmspeaker Rezmir favors them over all other types. Second, a detailed search coupled with a successful DC 10 Wisdom (Perception) check spots that many of the black dragon carvings have holes in their mouths.

A passage in the southwest corner of the shrine chamber leads to a chute that rises 30 feet up to area 11. A rope ladder is fixed at the top; a rug covers the opening.

Acid Trap

The holes in the dragons' mouths are nozzles for a trap that sprays acidic mist. The trap has two triggers. The first is under the chest in the northwest corner. If the chest is moved, the trap goes off. The second is in the chest. If it is forced open, or if the lock is inexpertly picked (a Dexterity result of 14 or less), the trap goes off.

> You hear a snap from beneath the chest, followed by a hissing sound like dozens of angry snakes—or like liquid moving through open tubes. A moment later, liquid sprays out from dozens of tiny holes in the walls and ceiling. Wherever it splashes onto the floor, the moisture on the stone bubbles and smokes. Within moments, the chamber is filled with acidic mist.

Everyone in the chamber must succeed on a DC 10 Dexterity saving throw or take 2d6 acid damage from the acid sprayed onto them (half as much damage on a successful saving throw). The real danger from the acid is not to the characters' skin, however, but to their lungs. Everyone must also succeed on a DC 10 Constitution saving throw or take 2d8 extra acid damage. Players who declare immediately that their characters are covering their faces and getting out of the chamber as quickly as possible, and are trying to not inhale the vapor, have advantage on their Constitution saving throws.

Treasure

The chest contains a few of the choicest items seized during the cult's recent treasure raids. Mondath persuaded Rezmir to let her keep them, and she promised to bring them with her when she travels north for the ceremony at the Well of Dragons. In truth, she wanted something to fall back on if everything went sour (she never mentioned that last part to Rezmir). Inside are a string of pearls (300 gp), a gold-and-sapphire ring (900 gp), and a pouch containing a half-dozen masterfully cut and polished precious stones (100 gp each). The ring and the pearls were taken from Greenest and would be recognized by anyone from there, but the stones came from elsewhere and would be difficult to identify. If the items from Greenest are returned, their owners will pay a reward worth 25 percent of their value (300 gp).

10. Dragon Hatchery

This chamber holds three eggs that Rezmir hoped to hatch into a new brood of dragons. They have not hatched yet but they will very soon, which is why Rezmir was unwilling to move them when the camp packed up and left. Instead, she left them under the care of Mondath and the kobolds. The chamber is dark; the kobolds extinguished their lights when they heard fighting in area 9.

> The chamber that opens at the bottom of the stairs is immense. A wide ledge runs along the left wall and drops away to a pit on the right. Many stalactites descend from the ceiling, and the sound of dripping water echoes continuously.

The lower portion of the room (10A) is 15 feet below the ledge. Wooden steps have been built down to the lower floor. As in room 7, the steps are enclosed in a stout iron cage with a gate at the bottom. The key to the gate hangs on a wall peg opposite the top of the stairs. As soon as characters advance into the room as far as the top of the stairs, they come under attack from the kobolds hiding in 10B. See that description for details.

From the ledge, characters can just make out the shapes of large eggs (each egg is nearly three feet tall) in the darkness below. The cavern extends into darkness beyond the range of their light. They need to go down the stairs and explore the area directly to discover its full extent. Characters standing along the ledge can discern many large, dark stains on the rough floor at the base of the ledge, but what caused them is not apparent.

10A. Black Dragon Eggs

This area is warm and humid. After characters look closely at the floor, they can determine that the stains are blood, and some of them are fresh. They come from the meat the kobolds toss down here.

Huddled in the shadows at the far edges of the room or behind the natural columns are two **guard drakes** trained to protect the dragon eggs. They don't attack as soon as characters come through the gate but wait until the characters have moved into the chamber. The drakes' first priority is to protect the eggs. Their second priority is to get between the intruders and the steps to prevent them from escaping. Unless characters climb down into 10A without using the stairs, they trigger the kobolds' attack before exploring this area.

Mixed in among the stalactites near the southeast corner of the room is an unusual **roper** that can speak Common. It doesn't attack the kobolds or guard drakes because the kobolds feed it spoiled meat that the guard drakes won't eat. If attacked, it fights back (and it's very dangerous to 3rd-level characters!). It can reach anywhere in area 10 with its tentacles, and it can also move at speed 10. It is currently full and curious about strangers, however, so it's not averse to talking. Its only real concern is food. If told about the supply of meat in area 6 and brought some as proof, it leaves the characters alone while it creeps away to investigate the larder.

A total of three dragon eggs are spread throughout the area. Each is about three feet tall and weighs 150 pounds. Two of them are easy to spot just by walking through the room with a light source. The third is tucked into a pile of similar-colored stones behind one of the columns, making it easy to miss. When characters search the room, have everyone make a Wisdom (Perception) check. Only a character who gets a 15 or higher notices the egg in its camouflaged nest. Looking at a dragon egg, a character can determine the color of dragon with a successful DC 10 Intelligence (Nature) check.

If the eggs are left here, they hatch in less than a week. If they are taken away, whether they hatch depends on how they are stored and treated. Away from a warm, humid environment such as this chamber, their progress halts until they are again in a suitable incubator. The dragons can be killed easily if the eggs are smashed,

crushed, or stabbed. If an egg is simply cracked open, the infant dragon struggles for breath, cries and squirms like a human baby for a few minutes, and then dies.

10B. Kobolds in Hiding

The floor of this area is about 10 feet below the ledge. The four **kobolds** who tend the eggs hid in this depression when they heard the fight break out in area 9. When characters approach within 25 feet of the ledge overlooking 10B (when they come in line with the top of the stairs to 10A), two kobolds toss glue bombs and the other two toss fire bombs. They do the same thing on the next round. Then they wait a round or two, if possible, while the roper in area 10A drags characters into its tentacles, bites them, or drops them 20 feet to the guard drakes.

Glue Bomb. Each creature within 10 feet of the bomb's target point must succeed on a DC 11 Dexterity saving throw or be restrained. The target or another creature within reach of it can use an action to make a DC 11 Strength check; if the check succeeds, the effect on the target ends.

Fire Bomb. Each creature within 10 feet of the bomb's target point must succeed on a DC 11 Dexterity saving throw or take 4 (1d8) fire damage (half as much damage on a successful saving throw).

If all else fails, the kobolds scramble up their makeshift ladder and attack with their shortswords.

11. Frulam Mondath's Chamber

Frulam Mondath (see appendix B) moved into this simple but comfortable chamber when the camp was abandoned. If no fight has occurred with the guards in area 12 and characters enter this chamber from area 9, then Mondath is here when they arrive. Guards in area 12 hear whatever happens in this chamber and respond dutifully.

The chamber contains a writing desk and stool, several tables with books

GUARD DRAKE

and papers, and a mirror on a floor stand. Light comes from two oil lamps. Thick rugs completely cover the floor, including an open chute that drops down to area 9. A rope ladder is fixed in the chute for climbing up and down, but nothing marks the position of the open, 3-foot-wide hole when it is covered by rugs. The slight depression it causes in the rug can be noticed with a successful DC 10 Wisdom (Perception) check. If someone steps on the chute without knowing it's there, the character must make a DC 10 Dexterity saving throw. Success means the character hops off the rug before it collapses through the hole, or grabs the top of ladder as he or she falls; failure means the character plunges 30 feet down the chute into area 9, taking 3d6 bludgeoning damage from the fall.

> Spread open on one of the tables is a simple map of the Greenfields area showing the villages the cult attacked and looted. An arrow is sketched in from the Greenfields toward the west and the town of Beregost on the Trade Way, where the arrow turns north. A separate sheet of paper that is covered with numerals in columns contains the note, "Everything must be freighted north to Naerytar. Rezmir allowed us to keep some pearls, a ring, and a handful of small stones." Other papers are of less interest; most of them have bad poetry about dragons.

The smaller chamber off the main one contains a bed, a trunk containing Mondath's clothes, and a second trunk containing Mondath's Cult of the Dragon regalia and a key to the chest in area 9. With this regalia, one person (preferably a human woman, but the clothing can be adjusted to fit a man) can be outfitted as a Wearer of Purple. It's worth noting that each Wearer of Purple's regalia is similar but unique, so high-ranking cult members are likely to recognize this regalia as Mondath's. When they see that the person wearing it is not Mondath, or if they know she is dead, alarm bells are guaranteed to go off.

Developments

If a fight breaks out in area 12 and four of the guards from that chamber retreat here to defend Mondath, her response is up to you. If the fight in the barracks takes a heavy toll on the characters, she might decide to confront them here. If the attackers plow through her forward guards, Mondath might retreat down the chute to area 9 and join forces with Cyanwrath or even flee from the cave. She has dedicated her life to the Cult of the Dragon, but she isn't eager to die for the cult. Mondath knows that the cult is amassing treasure in the north and that Rezmir spoke often of Tiamat, but that is the extent of her knowledge of the larger plan.

12. Guard Barracks

The guards who remained behind with Mondath use this chamber as their barracks. They maintain a two-person watch at the entrance (area 1); two dragonclaws are currently on duty in that area, and the others—three **guards** and eight **cultists**—are here, asleep or relaxing. If fighting against the dragonclaws from area 1 pushes near the passage to area 12, roll a d20; the guards here investigate the sound on a roll of 12 or higher. Otherwise they stay here, mostly oblivious to what's going on elsewhere.

If characters enter this chamber from area 2, the guards react quickly. Two of the guards and five of the cultists fight the characters here while one guard and three of the cultists retreat to area 11 to protect Frulam Mondath.

Treasure

The guards' scabbards are decorated with dragon motifs. They are worth about 5 gp each. They are not part of a Cult of the Dragon "uniform," but wearing one of these scabbards could buy a character credibility when trying to pose as a cultist. For example, you might grant a +1 bonus to Charisma checks made to fool or influence cultists. Aside from their gear, the guards have coins and small gems worth a total of 120 gp.

13. Treasure Storage

This chamber is now mostly empty, except for a few overturned boxes, broken items, scattered coins, small gems that were dropped during the hasty evacuation, and one **cultist** who is sleeping soundly on the floor after consuming several bottles of wine. He won't wake up from anything less than vigorous shaking, and it will be several hours before he is coherent. All the dropped items left in this room have a total value of only 16 gp.

Rewards

Award standard XP for defeated foes. This episode includes many challenges other than fights, and characters should be rewarded for overcoming them. The awards listed below are just recommendations; adjust them as you see fit. Characters might reach 4th level by the end of this episode, but it's not essential that they do.

- If you are using the milestone experience rule, the characters reach 4th level.
- For locating and disarming traps: 100 XP per trap.
- For offering the roper meat instead of fighting it to the death: 1,800 XP (the roper's standard XP value).
- For each dragon egg destroyed or taken: 250 XP.

With the dragon hatchery destroyed and the cultists all gone, characters should head for Elturel and their rendezvous with Leosin Erlanthar and Ontharr Frume. They might choose to follow the wagon tracks instead. The wagons followed the course roughly laid out on the map in Mondath's chamber: west to Beregost, then north along the Trade Way. They have at least a full day's head start on the characters, and possibly more, depending on how much time characters spent in Greenest before returning to the plateau.

EPISODE 4: ON THE ROAD

The treasure looted from the Greenfields is headed north on the Trade Way, hidden in unmarked freight wagons that are part of the regular merchant traffic of that well-traveled road. The heroes must find out where all that loot is going, which means taking a long, danger-filled trip northward.

The characters should travel from the abandoned cult camp southeast of Greenest to the city of Elturel on the River Chionthar. Their route takes them back through Greenest, where they can return any stolen goods that they recovered from the cult and recuperate from their wounds. Nighthill greets the characters with delight and respect. He tells them that before Leosin Erlanthar left town, he bought horses and riding gear for the characters to speed their journey to Elturel. The horses are being kept at the dealer's stables until the characters are ready to leave for Elturel; all their costs are paid for.

On horseback, characters can travel the 200 miles from Greenest to Elturel in about six days. They make the journey without incident, unless you throw an encounter or two at them to spice up the trip or to increase their XP totals. Encounters with bandits, humanoid clans, and roving monsters are appropriate in the untamed expanses of the Greenfields.

ELTUREL

Elturel, a large, orderly city overlooking the River Chionthar, is filled with merchants, river traders, and farmers' markets. Its most distinguishing feature is a brilliant magical light that hovers above it, illuminating it day and night. This light is painful to undead and is visible from almost every corner of Elturgard (of which Elturel is the capital), appearing from afar as a star or distant sun.

When the characters meet Ontharr Frume, they find him to be a good-natured paladin of Torm, the god of heroics and bravery. He is a man of action who loves jokes and pranks, a stiff drink, and a friendly scuffle.

If characters ask for Leosin Erlanthar when they arrive in Elturel, none of the locals know him. If they ask for Ontharr Frume, anyone can direct them to the "headquarters" of Frume's faction, the Order of the Gauntlet, at a tavern called A Pair of Black Antlers. If the characters arrive within a tenday of Erlanthar's departure from Greenest, then the monk is still there with his handful of disciples, too.

You can spend as much or as little time on interactions in Elturel as you and your players want. Characters are guaranteed to have a good time in Frume's company, provided they consider continual drinking, arm-wrestling, horseback riding contests, sparring, and weapon training to be a good time. If the players don't realize it, Erlanthar finds a quiet moment to be sure the characters understand that impressing Frume with their prowess, their honesty, and their drive is in their long-term interest. The characters can make a positive impression on Frume by winning a few contests (resolved quickly with opposed skill or ability checks) or sparring matches against his troopers or by telling entertaining tales of their exploits during the Greenest raid, in the raiders' camp, and in the dragon caves.

The Order of the Gauntlet

Late in the evening, after a day when Frume has been suitably impressed by the characters, he sends one of his squires to summon them to a private room in the tavern.

> Frume's squire shows you to a private space off the tavern's common room and closes the door when he leaves. Waiting for you in the room are the broad-shouldered human paladin, the monk Leosin, and many pitchers of dark red wine. The paladin's face wears a serious expression, unlike its usual open countenance.
>
> "My friends, we have important business to discuss. At this point, you know almost as much about it as we do, and thanks to you, we know twice as much today as we did a tenday ago. Something rotten is afoot. We have no formal organization to oppose these rascals—not yet anyway. We're working on that. And we need people like you, who know how and when to fight, and how and when to keep their heads down and observe. We can't promise you anything except long days filled with danger and stress—but what could be better than that, eh?"

Ontharr Frume and Leosin Erlanthar, along with a handful of other concerned leaders and scholars along the Sword Coast, are in the early stages of organizing against the Cult of the Dragon.

Erlanthar's organization is the Harpers. Characters might have heard of the older Harpers, but they're unlikely to know much about the secretive group beyond what is generally rumored: that the Harpers are dedicated to furthering equality and justice and to keeping power out of the hands of those who don't deserve it. Erlanthar explains that the Harpers are loosely organized; agents are allowed wide freedom of action.

Ontharr Frume represents the Order of the Gauntlet. His order shares many of the Harpers' principles, but the two organizations are very different. The Order of the Gauntlet emphasizes faith, vigilance, and constant struggle against threats of evil. Many of its members are clerics and paladins, but the order welcomes anyone who shares its ideals. Discipline is key, and the order is distinctly more structured and hierarchical than the Harpers.

The top concern of both groups is the Cult of the Dragon. In the past, the cult was more active to the east and it was focused on creating dracoliches. Its shift to the Sword Coast and new emphasis on living dragons

and on Tiamat are cause for concern. The cult is on the move and it's up to something big; the Order of the Gauntlet, the Harpers, and a third allied group known as the Emerald Enclave want to thwart the cult's plans.

In this meeting, Frume and Erlanthar are offering the characters the chance to join their factions. At this early stage, there is no pay for members and there are no ranks. What they can offer is help and support from other members and allies, who are spread from Nashkel and Candlekeep in the south to Neverwinter and Mirabar in the north. The horses that Erlanthar arranged for the characters are just one small example of the aid the Harpers and the Order of the Gauntlet can provide.

Harpers can be recognized by the group's symbol: a silver harp nestled between the horns of a crescent moon. Some people wear the symbol openly, and others keep it concealed. Erlanthar wears his as a medallion around his neck when he is certain that he's not heading into a potential captive situation—sometimes openly and sometimes tucked away. Members of the Order of the Gauntlet wear their holy symbols openly. (Frume's is the right-handed gauntlet of Torm.) The order's universal symbol is a gauntlet grasping a sword by the blade. Frume wears such a symbol on a pendant around his neck, hidden below his flowing beard.

Characters don't need to join either faction, but there are advantages to doing so and no real drawbacks. Even

ONTHARR FRUME

if characters don't agree to join, Frume and Erlanthar try to enlist their aid in tracking the cult's shipments.

THE MISSION

Thanks to the characters, the Harpers now know that the cult is amassing treasure and shipping it north. Where exactly this treasure is going and what the cult plans to do with it are the next two questions that need answering. Frume and Erlanthar would like the characters to join the cult's caravan and accompany it on the journey. They could get themselves hired as guards—if not by the cult's wagon masters, then by other merchants who are traveling in the same direction at the same time. Merchants from different companies commonly join together to form larger trains for protection. Frume has contacts among the many merchants of the region and is certain he can arrange a job.

Timing is an issue. The tracks leaving the cultists' camp and the map from Mondath's chamber both indicate that the wagons were heading west to pick up the Coast Way road, where they would turn north to Beregost and Baldur's Gate, a journey of about 550 miles. The wagons would take twenty-five to thirty days for that trip, depending on conditions. The wagons pulled out at least a day ahead of the characters' return to the camp, and the characters probably spent a day exploring the abandoned camp and clearing out the dragon hatchery. Returning to Greenest, resting, and traveling to Elturel account for eight to ten more days. Unless the characters walked to Elturel or lounged for days in Greenest before coming north, they should have at least ten to fifteen days before the cult's wagons reach Baldur's Gate.

The River Chionthar flows directly from Elturel to Baldur's Gate. A sailing vessel can make that trip downstream in about three days if it ties up overnight for safety, or two if it risks pushing on through the night by lamplight. Frume has already arranged for such a boat to leave at dawn the next morning. They are also provided with 50 gp each to cover expenses on the trip.

If the characters turn down this mission, Frume makes some remarks about how they aren't the people he thought they were, and he leaves the meeting more than a little bit angry. Erlanthar stays and makes one more appeal to their sense of honor and duty. If the characters still turn him down, he reaches into his tunic and pulls out a soft leather pouch, which he hands to one of the characters. Inside is a magnificent ruby worth 1,200 gp. He explains that if they take the mission, this ruby will be waiting for them in the hands of a Harper agent in Waterdeep.

That night, Frume sees that the characters are all equipped with new clothing and gear, and even new weapons if they want. He suggests that they change their appearance as much as they can in simple ways, to reduce the odds of anyone they might have met at the cult camp recognizing them.

The trip downriver to Baldur's Gate is uneventful, regardless of whether it takes three days or two. The characters can bring their horses along on the boat if they wish. The horses won't like it, but they'll manage.

BALDUR'S GATE

Baldur's Gate is a bustling center of trade, with goods coming from north and south by wagon along the Trade Way and by ship on the Sea of Swords, and from the east along the River Chionthar and from Cormyr and Sembia. Baldur's Gate is situated on a prominent bluff next to the river, overlooking an excellent natural harbor. It is divided into three distinct segments: the Upper City where the richest and most influential citizens live and where the city's marketplace (the Wide) is located; the Lower City, which surrounds the harbor and where most of the city's merchants live and conduct their business; and the Outer City, which lies outside the walls and where most of the city's laborers reside in conditions that vary from crowded but clean to squalid.

Depending on timing, characters might have just a few days to wait in Baldur's Gate, or up to a tenday. Most of that time should be spent contacting a merchant recommended by Frume and arranging affairs so they can spot the cult wagons when they arrive.

Frume's contact is a human trader named Ackyn Selebon. He operates an equipage business in the Outer City north of the city wall, in a district called Blackgate. There he sells all the material needed for long-distance freight hauling: wagons, rope, netting, grease, chains, wheels, and so on. His shop also repairs wagons. He is not directly involved in the hiring of guards for caravans, but he knows people who are. With him to vouch for the characters, they should have no trouble getting hired on as guards for a northbound caravan, but he can't give them work with a specific merchant.

HIRING OUT

Baldur's Gate doesn't allow wagons, pack animals, horses, or even dogs into the city. The streets are so narrow, steep, and slick from frequent rain that heavy wagons would be a menace. This is actually one of the reasons why Baldur's Gate is such a bustling commercial hub: for goods to pass through the city from south to north, for example, they must be unloaded in the Outer City east of the wall, carried through the city by porters on foot, and reloaded onto different wagons north of the city for the rest of their journey. No road conveniently bypasses the city—a situation that the gate's profiteering intermediaries work hard to maintain. Most merchants find it easier to sell their loads to those intermediaries and consignment dealers when they reach Baldur's Gate, buy a new load of exotic goods from somewhere far away, and turn around and head back home, where they can again sell the new goods at a profit.

Along with wagons, guards seldom make a continuous journey through Baldur's Gate. Guards for northbound caravans are typically hired in Blackgate where northbound wagons begin their journey. Selebon tells the characters that if they hang around any of the taverns or tent saloons near his shop, they are sure to see all the northbound traffic. They shouldn't hesitate to use him as a reference if a potential employer asks for one.

The northbound journey from Baldur's Gate is arduous, so merchants travel together for safety. Each merchant hires guards independently, but the common belief is that if everyone hires two or three and enough wagons travel together, the caravan is well protected.

Within a few days (the wait is up to you and the timing you've worked out for the cargo's arrival from the camp), characters spot people they recognize from the cult's camp on the plateau. Rezmir, being a half-dragon, can't travel openly in Baldur's Gate; she'd be attacked by a mob. The city's wealthy elite, however, often travel the streets in screened or curtained palanquins for both comfort and privacy. Rezmir does the same. When characters spot familiar faces from the cult camp, the cultists are carrying or accompanying a palanquin where Rezmir rides. They might catch a glimpse of her through a briefly parted curtain if they're observant.

Rezmir and her bodyguards come to Selebon's yard to purchase five wagons and supplies (having sold the other wagons south of the city). Once they are equipped, local porters pack merchandise and supplies onto the wagons, cover them in canvas, and lash them down.

After the characters have identified the cultists' wagons and seen their arrangements, they should have an easy time getting hired as guards. They can apply to the cultists if they feel like being reckless, but other merchants are making the same preparations to leave on the morrow. Select anyone from the list of merchants and travelers to be a potential employer. Each character makes a Charisma (Persuasion) or Strength (Athletics) check, whichever they prefer. Check the results below.

HIRING OUT

d20	Result
0–5	No one is interested in hiring the character, but he or she can tag along as a traveler. Guards sometimes quit or die on the road, and a replacement has a chance to find employment.
6–10	Hired as a basic guard for 5 gp per tenday, plus food and living expenses on the road.
11–15	Hired as a sergeant for 8 gp per tenday, plus food and living expenses on the road.
16+	Hired as a bodyguard for the merchant at 10 gp per tenday, plus food and living expenses on the road.

All hires are for the journey to Waterdeep. Sergeants are expected to manage two to five other guards. Bodyguards are expected to stick close to their employer and protect him or her against harm.

FELLOW TRAVELERS

During the course of this journey, the characters have opportunities to meet a range of people from across Faerûn. Merchants, mercenaries, pilgrims, scholars, thieves, and explorers all mingle on the great Trade Way.

KEY NONPLAYER CHARACTERS

Two NPCs who join the caravan partway through the trip are especially important: Azbara Jos and Jamna Gleamsilver. Both join the caravan at Daggerford, about 120 miles south of Waterdeep and the last place where the caravan takes a day-long rest. They are not traveling together; being in Daggerford at the same time is coincidental.

Azbara Jos (see Appendix B for statistics) is a male human and a Red Wizard of Thay. Red Wizards are widely disliked and mistrusted, so he takes some pains to disguise his membership in that group by always wearing a wool cap with ear and neck flaps to cover his shaved, tattooed head. It's not an especially effective disguise; characters who make a successful DC 15 Wisdom (Perception) check notice the edges of the tattoos peeking out from under the cap. Many Thayans have shaved, tattooed heads, however, but only a few are Red Wizards. Countless Thayans fled their country when the lich Szass Tam seized control, so they are not entirely strange on the Sword Coast. If questioned, Jos claims to be just another Thayan expatriot trying to find refuge while his country is controlled by undead monsters. In fact, other than the denial that he's a Red Wizard, this is all true.

Jos buys space aboard one of the cult wagons, although they turned away everyone else who sought passage earlier in the journey. He does not mingle with the other travelers and seldom speaks to anyone except the man who seems to be the leader of the cultists.

Jamna Gleamsilver (see Appendix B for statistics) is a female gnome and a member of a secretive organization called the Black Network, also known as the Zhentarim. Outwardly, the Black Network provides mercenaries and other forms of muscle for hire. Informally, it is known as a criminal society akin to a widespread thieves guild. Secretly, its leaders seek to extend their shadowy fingers into every throne room and ruling council chamber in Faerûn. Like the Harpers, the Zhentarim too are aware that the Cult of the Dragon is on the move, and they need to know the cult's plans so they can prevent them from interfering with the Zhentarim's own plans, plus perhaps take advantage of the plunder possibilities.

That's why Gleamsilver joins the caravan. The Black Network's spies learned that the cult is moving freight northward and, like the characters, she was tasked with finding out what they're hauling and where it's headed. Those above her seriously considered wiping out the caravan with mercenaries disguised as bandits, ransacking the wagons, and torturing cult members for the desired information. Fortunately for the characters, Gleamsilver persuaded her superiors to give her a shot at uncovering the truth in a less bloody fashion. If she hasn't come up with something useful by the time the caravan reaches Waterdeep, she will put plan B—the one involving mass murder—into action.

Despite the vast gulf between their outlooks, the Black Network and the Harpers have a common enemy, and that is pushing them into an unlikely alliance. Gleamsilver is the antithesis of a hero—she is self-serving, a skilled thief and liar, and willing to murder anyone who stands between her and her goal.

OTHER NONPLAYER CHARACTERS

This list of twenty NPCs is provided for when you need one quickly. You can, of course, change any details about them that you wish. Use them to flesh out the caravan, to spice up the journey, to help bring the trip to life, and to give characters people to like and protect, or dislike and quarrel with, along the way.

Achreny Ulyeltin (Male Human Merchant). Ulyeltin is an independent wagon master with two wagons in this caravan. Both are hauling cured furs and uncured hides. He is a boorish man without a trace of civilization about him. He's not unfriendly—just smelly, vulgar, and utterly without manners. His second wagon driver and two laborers, on the other hand, are perfectly pleasant.

Aldor Urnpoleshurst (Male Human Lawyer). A lawyer by training but a skunk by inclination, Urnpoleshurst is relocating from Baldur's Gate to anywhere that isn't Baldur's Gate. Gossip around the caravan is that he was driven out by a scandal, and that's hard not to believe. He is suspicious of everyone and makes outrageous accusations at the drop of a hat.

Beyd Sechepol (Male Half-Elf Merchant). Ale and beer are so common that not much money can be made hauling them long distances. But that's what fills Sechepol's wagon. He will make his money on the road, selling his stock to his fellow travelers in the caravan. He is diplomatic and has a gift for defusing arguments to everyone's satisfaction before they escalate to violence, but he is careless about gear and horses—a fault that can cause friction with those who hate to see a horse mistreated through thoughtlessness.

Edhelri Lewel (Female Moon Elf Merchant). Lewel's wagon is loaded with exotic wood from the Jungle of Chult for the master carpenters and cabinetmakers of Waterdeep to turn into exquisite furniture. She is the exact opposite of Beyd Sechepol in temperament: impatient with people but exacting about her wagon and doting on her animals.

Eldkin Agetul (Female Shield Dwarf Guard). Agetul has made this trip several times before and never hesitates to wave that experience in others' faces. She is a perfectionist, and she wants others to know it.

Enom Tobun (Male Lightfoot Halfling Teamster). Tobun has driven freight wagons across Faerûn for the past forty years, from Waterdeep to Calimport and from Baldur's Gate to Hillsfar. He is a font of stories and legends, but it's impossible to tell the truth from fiction in his tales. If anyone challenges him on the truth of a story, he grows argumentative, then sullen and vengeful. As long as a traveler stays on his good side, Tobun is a wonderful traveling companion.

Green Imsa (Female Human Traveler). The reason behind Imsa's name is obvious: she is green

AZBARA JOS

from head to foot. Her skin, hair, eyes, nails, teeth—everything about her is green. She readily admits that she is traveling to Waterdeep in search of a remedy for her condition. The coloration doesn't seem to bother her, but she becomes flustered if anyone asks how she came to be this way. She is friendly, if somewhat quiet, as long as the conversation stays away from her past.

Lai Angesstun (Male Gold Dwarf Merchant). This ambitious merchant is hauling scented cooking oil and perfumes from Amn, hoping to make a huge profit from the aristocrats and dandies of Waterdeep. He talks about money constantly: how much he intends to make, how he will spend it, and how others will envy him for it. He will not spend a single copper buying anyone else a drink or a roasted turnip during the entire trip.

Lasfelro the Silent (Male Human Merchant). From time to time, Lasfelro inexplicably breaks into merry songs and short stretches of joke-telling. His voice is a fine tenor and his jokes are hilarious. But these gregarious moods are always short. The rest of the time, he is silent as the grave, staring sullenly at the road ahead, barely moving on the seat of his wagon, seeming hardly to breathe. No one knows what he transports in his wagon, but it is guarded by a brooding gargoyle that is tethered to the wagon by a slim, silver chain.

Leda Widris (Female Human Guard). Widris is as honest and courageous as mercenaries come. She has spent many years in the south and now wants to see the snows and frozen seas of the far north and experience what a truly cold wind feels like.

Losvius Longnose (Male Lightfoot Halfling Teamster). Although Losvius's nose is respectably large, even for a halfling, the appellation Longnose was hung on him for a different reason: he is curious about everything, including other people's business, and especially other people's embarrassing secrets. Losvius doesn't poke his nose where it's not wanted in a search for blackmail material. He is just overpoweringly curious about what other people don't talk about. If he is along, there's a good chance one or more of the characters will find him nosing through their belongings when he thought their backs were turned.

Noohar Serelim (Male Moon Elf Merchant). Noohar and his mute brother, Selvek, are hauling exquisite wooden carvings made by the elves of Cormyr. Where his brother communicates only through sign language, Noohar may be the most articulate person the characters have ever met. Speech springs from him like music from the harp of Milil.

BRYAN SYME

The fact that he seldom has anything to say never seems to stop him from talking or others from listening.

Nyerhite Verther (Male Human Merchant). A load of Calishite silk will make Nyerhite Verther a rich man in Waterdeep, or so he believes. Sadly, he did not inspect his silk carefully when he bought it, and it's infested with worms. If anyone spots them and points them out to Verther during the trip, he becomes unhinged in his anger and grief.

Orvustia Esseren (Female Human Guard). Esseren grew up in the farmland outside Baldur's Gate, and this is her first trip more than two miles away from home. She is smart, tough, and talented with both spear and bow, but she knows nothing of the world beyond her aunt's farm or of people who deal dishonestly. Her aunt, a wise woman, believes this trip will be good for her.

Oyn Evenmor (Male Human Merchant). Evenmor is an independent wagon master hauling exotic birds to the lucrative markets in Waterdeep. He is a stubborn, argumentative man with strong opinions about almost everything, but he is generous when it comes to pouring drinks for those who will sit and argue with him endlessly.

Radecere Perethun (Male Rock Gnome Traveler). No one knows where Perethun is ultimately headed or why. He eats alone, seldom speaks, and always rides in the back of the wagon, staring wistfully at the road gone by. The only thing that brings him out of this shell is a game of chance. He gambles boisterously and well.

Samardag the Hoper (Male Human Merchant). Perhaps someone who hauls crates of expensive, fragile porcelain in a bouncing, jarring wagon along the Trade Way must be a born optimist. In Samardag's world, the sky is always blue, the weather is always fine, and the outlook for tomorrow is always bright. Odds are he would be a wealthy man if he hung onto his money, but he is a soft touch for every urchin and hard-luck story that crosses his path.

Sulesdeg the Pole (Male Human Guard). Among his tribe in his homeland of the Shaar, Sulesdeg's name means "tall as a lodge pole." On the Sword Coast, he is just known as "the Pole." At 7 feet 5 inches in height, he probably is the tallest human the characters or anyone else in the caravan has ever seen. He doesn't talk much, but when he does, people generally listen.

Tyjit Skesh (Female Shield Dwarf Guard). It won't take long before everyone in the caravan knows to steer clear of Tyjit Skesh. She is quick to anger and quicker to resort to her blades when something sets her off. She is honest to a fault and never fails to let people know why she was angry, so they can correct their behavior in the future. She will not tolerate bullying.

Werond Torohar (Female Human Teamster). Quiet, unassuming Werond Torohar can handle a team of horses or mules better than anyone on the Trade Way. She has an uncanny knack for making animals understand what she wants from them with only a twitch on the reins, a whistle, and a snap of her whip. Mud, stones, and ice seem to not be obstacles at all when Torohar is handling the team. She is a starry-eyed romantic at heart, and she can bring strong men to tears with her tales of long-ago lost loves and thwarted passion.

LIFE ON THE ROAD

The stretch of road from Baldur's Gate to Waterdeep is a journey of 750 miles. Horse-drawn or mule-drawn freight wagons cover 15 miles per day, depending on conditions. The animals need one day off after every six days of hauling to recover from their work. All things considered, the trip is expected to take two months.

The caravan leaving Baldur's Gate contains the three wagons of the Cult of the Dragon plus 2d4 more. Not all travelers are merchants. A wagon might carry a family relocating to the north or a diplomat on a mission to Waterdeep. People and wagons join the caravan along the way, and others leave according to the dictates of business and fortune. Some travelers ride horses, some walk beside the wagons, and some pay the merchants to ride aboard their wagons. On several occasions, characters notice the cult teamsters turning away passengers even though they have spare room on their wagons.

Nothing identifies the cult's wagons as anything but typical merchants hauling northbound freight. They don't bunch up during the day or camp together at night. As far as anyone else knows, their only connection is that they're part of this caravan.

Rezmir and eight of her guards leave Baldur's Gate secretly ahead of the caravan and ride north at a fast clip. They are headed for Castle Naerytar in the Mere of Dead Men and won't be seen again until episode 6. She leaves twelve **guards** behind. One travels with each wagon, acting as a guard and assistant to the teamster. The other nine are cloaked as private travelers in two distinct groups, seeking company and protection in the caravan for their journey.

The wagons travel for about eight hours per day, with a few stops to feed and water the horses and mules. Many nights are spent camping along the road. Most small towns have roadside inns if travelers want more comfort, and walled hostelries catering to wagon caravans are spread a few days apart. Animals and travelers can rest comfortably at these walled compounds while wagons are safely locked inside. The map for episode 5 shows a structure that once served that purpose. It can be used as the model for a typical hostelry if needed.

The most difficult part of the journey is near the beginning. A few days' travel north of Baldur's Gate brings the caravan into a countryside known as the Fields of the Dead. The road twists and wanders through hills dotted with ancient battlefields, dolmens, and barrow mounds. Common wisdom holds that it's a very bad idea to light a fire on a hilltop at night in the Fields of the Dead, because the light attracts monsters from miles around. Crossing this territory takes several days, during which everyone will be edgy and on watch.

RANDOM ROAD EVENTS

The journey north lasts about forty days, and most travelers hope these days are monotonous and uneventful. This being Faerûn, that's never the case.

Many days pass with no excitement, but others see monster attacks, strange incidents, excitement at roadside stops, meetings with NPCs, and the ever-present question of where the cult's wagons are headed. You can pace these events however you like. Use a few, use them all, or make up more of your own.

On a trip of this length, checking for random events every hour is excessive. The Trade Way sees a lot of travelers and it is relatively (if not entirely) safe. Check for a random event each day by rolling a d20. On a roll of 16 or higher, one or more events occur as indicated below:

- 16 means an event occurs in the morning
- 17 means an event occurs during the first rest stop
- 18 means an event occurs in the afternoon
- 19 means an event occurs in the evening or night
- 20 means one event occurs in the morning and another during afternoon or night

When an event occurs, select one that seems appropriate to the location, the timing, and the backstory that the characters have thus far, or you can roll a d12 to select one randomly. You can substitute a random bandit (daytime) or monster (nighttime) attack for any other event if a dose of instant action is needed.

Experience point awards for these events are up to you. We recommend 300 XP per character for each situation the heroes resolve successfully. Ideally, the characters have the chance to complete eight or nine of these events. If you use the milestone experience rule, the characters reach 5th level at the end of this journey.

TRADE WAY EVENTS

d12	Event
1	Adventuring Life
2	Animal Abuse
3	Bane of the Mountains
4	Contraband
5	Everything Has a Price
6	Fungus Humongous
7	The Golden Stag
8	Payback
9	No Room at the Inn
10	Roadside Hospitality
11	Spider Woods
12	Stranded

ADVENTURING LIFE

Another group of adventurers joins the caravan or is staying at the same roadside inn. Judging by their boasting, they have bested some of the most ferocious monsters and foes Faerûn has to offer. They look prosperous, they're filled with exciting tales, and they strike up a bond with a merchant who employs one or more of the characters. The next morning, that merchant informs the characters that their services are no longer needed because he has hired more experienced guards.

The newcomers are a troop of actors trying to pay their way to the next town. They are gambling that no danger will arise that needs them to step up and fight. When it does (as it surely will), it becomes painfully obvious that not one warrior or wizard is among them; they are five **human commoners** with charisma to burn and shiny stage props for weapons and armor. After they've been rescued from danger, the characters'

former employer, now suitably chastened, is willing to hire the characters back at slightly increased wages.

ANIMAL ABUSE

One of the travelers—a **noble**—is regularly seen mistreating his horses. He allows their collars and girths to chafe sores in their hide, skimps on their feed, and whips them when the aching, hungry animals don't pull hard enough or fast enough to suit him. If the characters still have their horses, he admires them and offers to buy one or more to replace the "useless nags" he is stuck with. Eventually, one of his horses will collapse in its harness, and he will either beat it to death in the road or cut it loose and leave it to die, unless one or more characters intervenes. He has a **knight** and a **mage** traveling with him as bodyguards.

BANE OF THE MOUNTAINS

High above, two **perytons** are watching the road for fresh hearts they can consume before laying their eggs. They circle at an altitude where they are easily mistaken for eagles. Each character can make a DC 15 Intelligence (Nature) check upon seeing the creatures. Success means they recognize the perytons for what they are before the first dive attack. Failure means the character is surprised.

CONTRABAND

One of the cult wagons overturns on a difficult corner or when a wheel breaks on a rock. Of the crates that tumble free, one smashes open, revealing dozens of beautiful items of jewelry wrapped in wool for protection. This is an excellent opportunity for the characters to see some of the contraband and even to get friendly with the cultists by helping them repair their wagon.

The cult members are angry that people saw the contents of their spilled cargo. Their instructions, direct from Wyrmspeaker Rezmir, were to keep the material secure and secret. Witnesses who show much interest in the jewelry or who ask questions might need to be silenced. NPC witnesses could disappear overnight or die unexpectedly from sudden illness (which a successful DC 10 Wisdom [Medicine] check reveals to be poison). The same attacks can be directed against characters who show too much curiosity.

EVERYTHING HAS A PRICE

Someone in the caravan develops a fancy for a treasured possession that belongs to one of the characters. The NPC tries to buy it, but the offered price is low. The NPC persists through the day, becoming more obnoxious without getting any more generous. Unless the character takes special precautions, the object disappears overnight. If the character accuses the NPC publicly the following morning, they make an enduring enemy; that NPC doesn't have the item and is incensed at the accusation. Someone else who witnessed the conversations the day before decided the other NPC provided perfect cover for a little nighttime thievery and took the missing item. To find the item, characters need to surreptitiously search people's bags and wagons, since few people will agree to have their belongings rifled through as if they were common thieves—especially not a common thief.

Fungus Humongous

After two days and nights of rain, lightning, and strange whistling sounds on the wind, characters awaken to see that the surrounding countryside is blanketed with fungus. It grows everywhere, including on the road. When anyone steps on a mushroom (it's nearly impossible not to), it emits a puff of black spores and a moan of pain. These tiny shriekers sprout from an immense mycelium that has spread beneath the area from shallow caves. They can be identified with a successful DC 15 Intelligence (Nature) check, but if the roll is 10–14, the character misidentifies them and believes they are deadly poisonous (they aren't).

The merchants are terrified of the things and refuse to drive through them, fearing that they may be poisonous or worse. Besides that, the sounds spook the animals and make them impossible to control.

The mushrooms are growing so fast on the rain-soaked ground that a person can almost see them getting bigger. They were the size of champagne corks when first noticed; within an hour, they grow six inches tall, and a foot tall an hour later. Their growth slows down after that, but by then, most people in the caravan are certain that all is doomed.

Anyone can literally sweep a path through the mushrooms with a heavy broom, a scythe, or a tree branch. The noise is distressing. Everyone involved in this process must make a DC 10 Constitution saving throw. Failure means the character is overcome with feelings of grief and remorse, seemingly triggered by hearing thousands of tiny cries of pain and death groans but which is in fact the result of inhaling mildly toxic spores released by the immature fungi. Affected characters break down after 1d20 minutes and simply can't face those sounds anymore. They have nightmares for days to come, until the toxin is completely out of their system. You can impose even more lingering results if you like, such as a lifelong aversion to eating mushrooms of any kind.

People can clear a path through the mushrooms with six man-hours of work (six people could do it in one hour, or three people could do it in two hours).

The Golden Stag

On a beautiful, sunny afternoon, a herd of **deer** is spotted grazing on a nearby hill. The travelers take such opportunities to hunt fresh meat for the larder. This herd, however, includes a magnificent stag (use **elk** statistics) that shimmers in the light as if its coat is spun from gold and its antlers plated with platinum. Nearly everyone in the caravan who can handle a bow wants to bring down that beast. Its pelt would be worth a fortune, even if it's not real gold. A few of the more cautious types warn that the creature is clearly a blessed being and that killing it would bring bad luck on the caravan, but no more than two or three people are persuaded. In minutes, the hunt is on, and the deer herd scatters into the nearby forest and through farmers' fields.

The characters can join the chase, try to talk people down, protect the stag, or ignore the situation, as they see fit. It can be tracked through the forest with a successful DC 10 Wisdom (Survival) check. A new check must be made every 500 yards.

The stag leads hunters on a 1,500-yard chase (three Wisdom (Survival) checks) to a moss-grown, ivy-draped ruin in the forest. There, one of three things can happen. Choose the one that best suits your game.

- The stag can be cornered, fought, and killed. It is a normal stag but with a breathtakingly beautiful coat of golden fur. If the local farmers learn that it's been killed, they grab their pitchforks and longbows and threaten to overrun the caravan unless they are paid 500 gp for their loss; the stag brought them luck.
- The stag greets the characters in Sylvan. If none of the characters speak that language, it switches to Elvish, and if no one responds again, it tries heavily accented, pidgin Common. It assures them that they are on the right track, and they must continue following the river of gold until they reach the castle in the sky. Sadly, their path will be filled with hardship and blood. To aid them, it offers the character a +1 longbow. The bow appears on the ground before them, and then the stag fades from view saying, "Not all will survive . . ."
- When the characters search the tumbled ruins, they find no sign of the stag but see a thin person who resembles a wood elf with bright golden skin. The young male is naked and either is wearing an antlered headpiece or has delicate antlers growing from his head. He drops to his knees and beseeches the characters in a dialect of Elvish that is archaic but understandable. He is an elf prince, and the stones around them were once the beautiful castle where he ruled. But he was cursed by the father of the woman he loved to transform into a golden stag whenever he steps outside these walls. He has lived with the curse for so long that his kingdom is forgotten, his castle is fallen to ruin, and he no longer remembers his own name. He believes that a wizard somewhere can release him from the curse, but wherever he goes, people try to kill him for his golden coat. If the characters allow him to accompany them and protect him, he will do his best to reward them at the end of the journey. The story is true; several wizards in Waterdeep could remove the curse. The elf cannot pay a reward at the end, but the characters earn 500 XP apiece for believing him and protecting him. That job won't be easy, because people in the caravan find their story ridiculous and look for opportunities to kill the stag.

Payback

As the caravan rounds a bend in the road, a human head can be seen sitting in the middle of the road a hundred yards ahead. From a distance, characters with a passive Wisdom (Perception) score of 15 or higher recognize that the head is actually a person buried up to the neck, and he is unconscious but still alive. That fact is obvious to anyone who approaches within 10 yards, as is the word "Oathbreaker" painted on his forehead.

The buried human is in bad shape from exposure and dehydration. Any healing magic or some water and a successful DC 10 Wisdom (Medicine) check revives him.

Many of the merchants in the caravan are of the opinion that whoever this is, if someone or something went to the trouble of marking him as a traitor and burying him up to the neck in the Trade Way, he probably deserves it and should be left there. If characters are working as guards for NPC merchants, at least one of their employers is among this group. It's obvious from wheel tracks on the turned-over earth that other wagons have indeed passed him by during the last few days.

Digging the man out of the ground takes two diggers at least two hours, and refilling the hole takes another hour (you can't just leave a hole in the road).

The buried man is Carlon Amoffel. He is a human **spy** and a member of the Harpers; characters discover a Harper tattoo on his arm if they dig him up. He has nothing but the loincloth he was buried in.

Publicly, Amoffel's story is that the oath he broke was a promise to marry a woman. He broke the engagement because he discovered that her father and brothers were all bandits and that he was expected to join them.

If any of the characters are Harpers and they reveal their association to Amoffel, he tells them the real story. He was on exactly the same mission they are: tracking a shipment of stolen loot north. But the smugglers—he's sure they're members of the Cult of the Dragon— became suspicious of him. Amoffel passed information to another Harper at a roadside inn, and members of the caravan witnessed the meeting. The cultists manufactured a story that he was passing information to bandits. The merchants were unwilling to kill him outright, but they were willing to leave him buried in the road and "let providence decide the man's fate."

Amoffel has Harper contacts in Waterdeep and knows his way around the city. He can be a useful ally when this caravan reaches its destination.

No Room at the Inn

After a miserably wet, cold day that promises to become an even wetter, freezing night, the caravan arrives at a large inn. Upon entering the warm, comfortable common room to make arrangements for the night, the embarrassed innkeeper tells the characters that the entire inn is sold out; all the private rooms are taken and the common room is reserved for a private party. The caravan will need to spend the night outside. Looking around the room, the characters see just one group: an aristocratic judge and his entourage of three human dilettantes. They smirk at the characters while making comments such as "sleep tight" and "have a pleasant evening" followed by insults muttered under their breath about the characters' mud-spattered clothing and low breeding. If characters ask about sleeping in the stable, one of the nobles speaks up, saying, "Our horses are rather picky about who they share space with. We had to reserve all of it, too, for their sake. You understand, I'm sure." His snooty friends have a good chuckle over that.

Spending this night in the wagons will be hard on the characters but will be misery for the unprotected horses and mules, and the only reason for it is the cruelty and arrogance of these snickering twits in the inn.

The NPCs in the inn won't be influenced by any sort of reason or debate or by offers of money. They find the situation enormously amusing and seem pleased by the prospect of the merchants and their animals suffering in the freezing rain all night. They needle and goad the characters and their fellow travelers at every opportunity, including from the doorway and windows of the inn when no one else is inside. If the characters don't start a fight, someone else from the caravan might.

In fact, these NPCs are four disguised **veterans** traveling to Baldur's Gate in search of employment and out to have a good laugh over someone's misfortune. They drop all pretense after violence breaks out.

Roadside Hospitality

When the caravan reaches its stopping point for the night, two buxom twin sisters are there ahead of them, setting up camp and tending to their horses. Arietta and Zelina Innevar take a liking to some of the travelers—possibly, but not necessarily, a few of the characters—and spend the evening asking about their past, where they're headed, whether they have family, and so on. The sisters are actually two **doppelgangers**. They can either attack someone that night or join the caravan for a few days while they study the travelers and choose their victims. When the time comes to strike, they wait until after dark, then try to lure their target away from other people by calling for assistance in a familiar voice. Fortunately for the characters and their fellow travelers, if one is defeated, the other one flees in a flurry of curses and vengeful threats.

Spider Woods

The Trade Way skirts around and between the huge Trollbark and Misty Forests, but it passes through many other, smaller forests that don't appear on maps. When the caravan is passing through one such wooded region, three **ettercaps** and two **giant spiders** attack it. They are chiefly interested in taking horses, not merchandise, but they won't balk at taking people if they can't get horses. Two ettercaps go after horses while the third ettercap and the giant spiders keep the caravan guards busy. An ettercap can cut a horse free from its harness in 3 rounds. After that, they retreat into the trees, leading the horse away with reins of webbing. Without horses, the wagons are stranded. The characters' employer insists they go after the ettercaps and retrieve the stolen horses.

If the characters move quickly, they have a good chance to retrieve the horses alive. The animals leave a trail through the underbrush that's easy to follow; a successful DC 10 Wisdom (Survival) check is sufficient to keep on it. The horses are led away about half a mile to the ettercaps' lair. If characters charge straight in, they are attacked by three **ettercaps** and two **giant spiders**. If they pause to observe for a few minutes, they see the ettercaps shoo the giant spiders away while they prepare for their feast of horse meat. The characters can then fight just the ettercaps for 6 rounds, before the spiders return to the sound of battle. The characters can't delay for long, however, because the ettercaps won't waste much time before killing and tucking into the horses.

STRANDED

This is an ideal event for the Fields of the Dead region, if one occurs there, but it can be used anywhere.

The caravan sees a fight happening ahead. A freight wagon is stranded on the road, its draft animals dead. A merchant (**noble**) and three **guards** are sheltered under the wagon, with crates dragged between the wheels for cover. They are plentifully supplied with crossbows and bolts, but the six **hobgoblins** and one **hobgoblin captain** assailing them seem content to keep them under siege until sundown, when they plan to rush the wagon with darkness as cover. These are Urshani hobgoblins, recognizable by their unusually savage appearance (even for hobgoblins). Urshani hobgoblins adorn themselves with wolf furs, paint worg heads onto their shields, and incorporate other wolf parts and icons in their armor and clothing.

First the hobgoblins must be driven off, then the injured attended to, and then something must be done about the stranded wagon. The trader has money to buy more horses if anyone is willing to sell. Otherwise, he'll take a lift to the next hostelry, where he can buy animals, while his three guards stay behind.

JAMNA GLEAMSILVER

automatically, for the sake of using this event.

If a character is recognized, allow that character to make a DC 15 Wisdom (Insight) check. Success means the character catches a cultist watching him or her suspiciously, noting who the character talks to, when the character eats, and where the character sleeps. Over the course of a few days, it should become obvious that this cultist has recognized the character. If characters delay taking action, the cultists strike first by trying to assassinate the characters in their bedrolls or perhaps by arranging an accident—a loose wheel, broken axle, or spooked lead horse might be an effective way to solve a problem. The only permanent solution to this problem for the characters is murder; the cultist with suspicions must be eliminated before he or she shares those suspicions with the others. Good characters may be reluctant to take this step; that's roleplaying. If they can find another way, that's excellent, but once the opposition recognizes someone, the situation is likely to end in death.

BRYAN SYME

PLANNED ROAD EVENTS

After Jamna Gleamsilver and Azbara Jos join the caravan, three planned events must take place. Their timing is up to you.

RECOGNIZED!

If the characters spent much time wandering through the raiders' camp on the Greenfields and talking to cultists, they might have struck up a conversation there with a cultist who is now one of the wagon drivers. Have each character make a Charisma check on the first day of the journey, but don't tell players what it's for. At some point during the journey, the character who scored the lowest result on the Charisma check is recognized by a cultist. The cultists assume that, at best, the character must be a deserter from the cult. At worst, he or she is a spy and a saboteur. At a dramatic point on the journey, when the caravan is away from Baldur's Gate, this means trouble.

Optionally, you can dispense with this die roll and have someone recognize one of the characters

UNWANTED ATTENTION

The day after the caravan leaves Daggerford, have each character make a Wisdom (Insight) check. (Alternatively, you can allow a Charisma [Deception] check here, permitting characters to use their knowledge of deception to recognize when someone else is putting the same talent to use. Only characters with training in Deception can choose this option.) Interpret the results as follows.

- 9 or less: The character notices nothing.
- 10–12: The character notices that the gnome who recently joined the caravan shows an interest in the human who joined at the same time and who was welcomed aboard one of the cult wagons as a passenger. They aren't together, but during stops, the gnome often sidles up near enough to overhear anything the human might say, and she has also been spotted hovering near the cult wagons when the cultists are busy with tasks other than guarding the wagons closely.
- 13–15: The character notices that the gnome shows an interest in the characters. She has spoken to several of them, asking innocuous questions and

commenting on the weather. She leaves the impression of being someone who flawlessly takes in every detail about people and her surroundings.

- 16+: The character notices both and has the impression that Gleamsilver is aware of the characters watching her, too.

If someone reveals a Harper badge to Gleamsilver, she responds with a curt "put that away, fool," and leaves.

WHO'S YOUR FRIEND?

On the morning of the day when the caravan is four days' travel from Waterdeep (two days after "Unwanted Attention"), Gleamsilver approaches the characters just as they are sitting down to the morning meal. After glancing around to make sure none of the cultists are watching, she puts her fingers to her lips, then takes the bowl of oatmeal that one of them is about to eat.

> After poking through your oatmeal with the blade of her dagger, the gnome lifts it out and shows you an oatmeal-smeared object resembling a tiny bead. She glances over her shoulder toward where cultists sit at their breakfast. "It's a sliver of bone," she whispers, "curled into a circle so you can swallow it in a mouthful of gruel without noticing. Once eaten, it slowly uncurls inside you, exposing needle points that pierce your guts and kill you slowly. I suspect they're in all your breakfasts." As she gets up and walks away, she adds, "Let's talk this evening."

No more bone slivers are in the characters' gruel. The one Gleamsilver showed them was already stuck to the underside of her dagger before she poked it into the bowl. If characters dig through their oatmeal looking for slivers, let them make DC 15 Intelligence (Investigation) checks. If a check succeeds, tell them they find several small lumps that might be bone slivers, but they might just as easily be oat husks, sawdust, or insect eggs. Also tell them that two of the cultists keep looking in their direction but appear to be trying to hide their interest.

That evening, after most of the travelers have bedded down, Gleamsilver comes to the characters. She begins by introducing herself if that hasn't happened previously. Otherwise, she gets right to the point.

> "We don't work for the same people, but we're all on the same side—we share a belief that the Cult of the Dragon must be stopped. I need to know what they're carrying in those wagons and where they're taking it. Will you help me find out? We can do it tonight."

If the characters tell Gleamsilver what they know about the cult's cargo, she expresses gratitude and relief that she doesn't need to risk breaking into their wagons. In fact, she already knows, but she needed to find out what the characters know. She pumps them for every bit of information they're willing to share while offering little in return except confirmation of what they already know. If the characters haven't figured out that Azbara Jos is a Red Wizard of Thay, she points that out and raises the question of why a Red Wizard is chumming it up with Cult of the Dragon members.

Gleamsilver is especially cagey about why she's interested in all this. The gnome never mentions the Zhentarim or the Black Network. She never comes out and says she works for the Harpers, either. Gleamsilver is an expert at picking up on the subtlest clues and using them to seem to know things she doesn't actually know and to say what people want or expect to hear. She uses that talent to great advantage against the characters in all their dealings. If players ask to use Wisdom (Insight) to detect whether the gnome is telling the truth, let them make the check. On a roll of 15 or higher, the character suspects Gleamsilver isn't telling them everything but doesn't discern an actual lie. On any other result, the characters detect no dishonesty.

MURDER MOST FOUL

Two days after "Who's Your Friend?" happens, the camp awakens to a killing. One of the cultists acting as a wagon guard was murdered overnight. He was stabbed in the back with a sword (the wound is too big to be from a dagger) and left where he fell beneath a cult wagon.

The dead man's companions immediately accuse one of the characters and demand to inspect the characters' weapons. If the character carries a shortsword, it will be a match, although that proves nothing. Any sword that size would be close enough. Many footprints are around the wagon, but a successful DC 10 Intelligence (Investigation) check determines that they are all from people crowding around the body in the morning. The ground was swept during the night to remove prints.

By this point in the journey, the characters should be popular with the other travelers; they probably have saved numerous lives and the entire caravan more than once. The cultists, on the other hand, are not so popular. They are standoffish and even a bit odd. This works in the accused character's favor, because many people will speak up in his or her defense.

If a character suggests that the wagon's owners should open their crates to see if anything is missing, the accusations die away. (If a character doesn't suggest this, an onlooker in the crowd does.) Uncharacteristically, Azbara Jos comes forward and tries to calm the situation, in the process saying more than anyone has so far heard him say at one time.

In the end, the caravan's most prominent merchants agree that without witnesses, nothing can be done. The gods will punish the guilty party and life will go on.

Most of the cultists never again look at the accused character with anything but undisguised hatred. This animosity becomes important later on in episode 5.

The murderer was, of course, Jamna Gleamsilver. Knowing what was in the cargo, she couldn't resist helping herself to some. The theft itself is undetectable, because she left no signs, and the cult isn't carrying a manifest of its looted treasure. The guard interrupted her in the act and had to die; it was just that simple.

EPISODE 5: CONSTRUCTION AHEAD

The freight travels as far north as possible, following the Trade Way past Waterdeep to where the great road was swallowed up by the ever-expanding Mere of Dead Men. A fortified roadhouse that once served merchants and teamsters now feeds laborers and safeguards road-building supplies, and it also aids the Cult of the Dragon in smuggling its treasure.

WATERDEEP

When the caravan rolls into Waterdeep after two months on the road, most of the merchants disperse to the city's markets, warehouses, and stables. They've reached their destination and the characters are paid off in silver and thanked for their service. If they performed well, they're told they can find work with these shippers any time in the future. Characters can't waste much time closing accounts with their own employers or sight-seeing in Waterdeep, however, or they lose the treasure wagons in the crowded metropolis.

The cult wagons don't follow the same pattern as the others from the caravan. Instead, they head for the north side of the city before looking for a place to spend the night. Everyone who the characters know to be associated with the cult gathers at the same spot by nightfall.

Azbara Jos remains with the cultists during this time, and Jamna expresses her desire to stick with the characters until they uncover the treasure's destination.

The cultists spend a day resting their horses at a stable on the north side of Waterdeep. Other wagons are already there, covertly carrying treasure from all over the Sword Coast to the collection point. During the day, some of the cultists visit a large warehouse just inside the northern city gate, where construction supplies are stockpiled for shipment north and where wagons are gathered and loaded for the trip.

If characters ask around Waterdeep's northern gate about anyone matching Rezmir's description, they hear rumors of a half-dragon being sighted in the area at least a tenday ago. Everyone remembers the incident; chromatic half-dragons are almost never seen, and they tend to cause alarm when they are. If the rumor is true, then the half-dragon was traveling with a strong escort of mounted guards, headed north. The rumor is true, of course, but it can't be confirmed 100 percent.

By asking around, characters learn that the road to the north, called the High Road, used to connect Waterdeep to the city of Neverwinter. A cold, coastal marsh called the Mere of Dead Men lay between the road and the coast. Over the years, the mere continually expanded. Each time it grew, it flooded the road, which had to be relocated farther inland. That was the situation until a century ago, when Neverwinter was nearly destroyed by the eruption of Mount Hotenow. With the city in ruins, efforts to keep the road open simply stopped. It no longer served a purpose.

But now, Lord Neverember is rebuilding Neverwinter and the road is needed again. The warehouse visited by the cultists is where shipments of supplies to the road-building camps are coordinated. If freight haulers went there, it must have been to see if they could haul supplies to the road-head for pay. Are they hiring guards for supply caravans? Sure, you bet they are. The Mere of Dead Men is wild and dangerous. Lord Neverember's agents in this endeavor are perpetually looking for laborers to build the road and fighters to protect the laborers. Turnover in those jobs is pretty high.

Northbound, Again

The characters have no trouble getting hired as wagon escorts at the supply warehouse. Unlike in the caravan, guards are not hired by individual wagon masters but by the High Road Charter Company, a consortium of guilds and noble houses partnered with Lord Neverember. A human **veteran** named Ardred Briferhew commands the entire convoy. It consists of six supply wagons, twelve escorts (including the characters and Jamna), and two dozen laborers marching out to relieve a group that is coming back to Waterdeep for some time off. Those cultists who weren't hired as teamsters for their three wagons are coming along as laborers.

The cultists are not happy to see the characters again, so the characters are the target of dirty looks.

The work camp the convoy is headed toward lies 200 miles up the coast. For most of that distance, the road winds through rough coastal hills nestled between the Sword Mountains and the sea. On the seventh night, the convoy camps on a hilltop from which characters have their first sight of the Mere of Dead Men. It is a chill tangle of trees, brush, boggy ground, standing water, reeds, and cat-tails stretching farther than the eye can see. The rest of the trip is within sight of the mere. The destination is reached sometime on the tenth day.

Encounters North of Waterdeep

Nothing much needs to happen on the trip north of Waterdeep. You can narrate through it quickly. At your option, use the random encounters below to spice up the journey. Roll a d20 each day and use the indicated encounter. Add 2 to the roll on days 8, 9, and 10.

Remember that the characters are just part of the convoy escort. The monsters listed on the Encounters North of Waterdeep table are those the characters must fight. At the same time, NPC members of the escort are dealing with additional monsters not listed here. Assume that monsters and the travelers are being alert before these encounters. After each encounter, roll 1d4 − 2. The result is the number of NPC escorts killed elsewhere in the battle.

Encounters North of Waterdeep

d20	Encounter
1–14	No encounter
15	12 human bandits
16	1 troll
17	4 orcs and 1 ogre
18	2 ogres
19	3 lizardfolk and 3 giant lizards
20	6 lizardfolk
21	8 giant frogs
22	12 bullywugs

Carnath Roadhouse

The convoy's destination is the Carnath Roadhouse, a compound that served as a hostelry on the trade road between Waterdeep and Neverwinter in the days when trade flourished. It fell into disuse when trade stopped, but now that the road is being rebuilt, the roadhouse has been repaired and put to use as a supply depot and wagon park. This part of the adventure plays like a spy story. Stealthy characters should find plenty to do here.

Essential Ingredients

The work camp is exactly what it appears to be: a supply depot for the road builders. It is also something more, however: a transit point for the cult's contraband coming up from the south.

When wagons arrive from the south, they are brought into the compound one or two at a time for unloading, then moved back outside for parking. The compound is crowded with food, lumber, and myriad other supplies in crates and barrels. Material that can't be left exposed to the cold, wet weather or is especially valuable is stored in the warehouse (area 3), and anything valuable is kept in the locked strong room attached to the warehouse (area 4). Only the camp superintendent, a burly **half-orc** known only as Bog Luck, has a key to that inner room.

Bog Luck was recruited to the Cult of the Dragon years ago. The only outward sign of this is the scabbard of his ever-present shortsword, which is decorated with a dragon resembling the designs on the scabbards characters saw in the dragon hatchery (and possibly have with them still; see area 12 in that section). When cult wagons arrive, their road-building cargo is unloaded into the compound normally, but Bog Luck ensures that the contraband is stored in the strong room. Afterward, he goes into the strong room alone and paints a symbol onto each carton belonging to the cult.

In the floor of the strong room is a camouflaged trapdoor. It can be found with a successful DC 10 Wisdom (Perception) check. The trapdoor connects to a dripping, slimy tunnel that runs 500 yards into a dense stand of trees and brush at the edge of the Mere of Dead Men. At night, when everyone in the compound is asleep except for a few rooftop guards, lizardfolk creep through the tunnel and take the marked crates to a location in the mere (the subject of episode 6). They seldom perform this task over a single night unless the shipment is very small. Typically they take one night per wagon.

1. Courtyard

Most of the time, this open courtyard is crowded with crates, barrels, and stacks of supplies. The damp climate means that the ground is muddy, except when the temperature is below freezing. Then the mud hardens into uneven, frost-covered ruts. A path is kept clear from the gate to the stables so animals can be moved, but during busy times, that path often runs under the balcony in front of the doors to the rooms.

2. Stables

In some ways, the stables are the most comfortable area of the compound. When the stables are crowded, the horses' and mules' body heat keeps the building warm. Four stable boys take care of the animals and sleep here. Only the youngest, a quick-witted boy called Wump, has any suspicion that something mysterious is going on. He knows nothing about the Cult of the Dragon, but he's sharp enough to wonder why anything used by the road builders needs to be locked up.

3. Warehouse

The warehouse door is latched but unlocked. Supplies that shouldn't be left exposed to the weather are stored here: food for the people and fodder for animals.

4. Strong Room

Unusually valuable cargoes and personal items are kept in the strong room under lock and key. None of the workers know or care what sorts of road-building supplies are considered so valuable they must be locked up for protection. They just follow Bog Luck's instructions and stack things where they're told to stack them.

Since the sleeping rooms can't be locked, workers and teamsters often have Bog Luck lock their cash and other valuables into the strong room for safekeeping. He keeps a record in a ledger book of all the personal items stored there and has a reputation for being meticulous about making sure everyone gets their belongings back—all of their belongings and *only* their belongings.

The key for this room is always on Bog Luck's belt, but the lock can be opened with a successful DC 10 Dexterity check and a set of thieves' tools.

The trapdoor is located in the southeast corner of the room. An empty crate nailed onto the door covers it; when the door is opened, the whole crate tips toward the north. Being nailed to the floor, the crate feels solid and full to a casual bump or shove. Only when it's tipped does the trick become obvious. It can be discovered with a thorough 20-minute search of the room or with a successful DC 10 Wisdom (Perception) check.

If characters search the strong room during the night, lizardfolk show up to cart away contraband. There are three **lizardfolk** for every two characters.

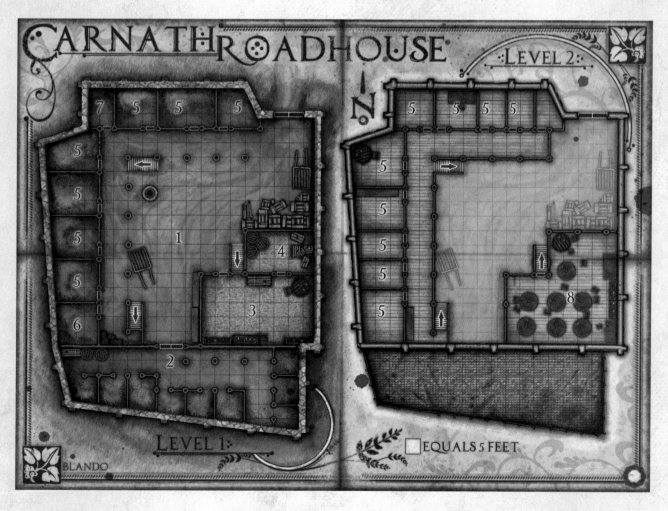

5. Rooms

The wagon drivers, escorts, and laborers who stay at the compound share the rooms. None are private rooms; all have bunks for at least four people, and the larger rooms sleep six. They contain bunks, trunks for belongings, and wooden floors covered with rushes.

None of the rooms have locks on their doors except Bog Luck's. If asked about locks, Bog Luck explains that they kept freezing in cold weather so people couldn't get into or out of their rooms. This excuse is credible; the upper room doors, in particular, often are coated with ice in the morning. In fact, Bog Luck removed the locks to strengthen his excuse for locking the strong room.

6. Bog Luck's Room

Bog Luck has this room to himself, so it's more spacious and comfortable than the others. He's seldom here except when sleeping, and he keeps the door locked. A successful DC 10 Dexterity check with thieves' tools can open it. Despite his crude manner, Bog Luck is a somewhat educated man, as evidenced by the books of philosophy and natural history on his reading shelf.

7. Ardred Briferhew's Room

The commander of the hired guards has this small room to himself. There is nothing remarkable about it.

8. Kitchen

This upper room is used for preparing food on a large stove. In the evenings, this doubles as a common room where people gather to smoke, drink, swap stories, and keep warm. Eventually the cook, a grumpy human called Gristle Pete, kicks everyone out so he can unroll his mattress and blankets and get some sleep.

If characters listen carefully to Gristle Pete's mutterings as he works around his kitchen, they'll hear him talking in circles to himself about how he ". . . don't get no sleep from all the critters in the floors banging and knocking and hissing and whispering at all hours" and so on. The noises he hears and mistakes for rats are the lizardfolk retrieving contraband from the strong room below. If questioned, he hears the noises every now and then, not every night. If pressed, he realizes that the sounds happen a few nights after a new load gets dropped off. Now ain't that some oddball rat behavior?

Tracking the Load

Characters have a few ways to collect clues about what's happening at the work camp. Jamna can help out with these tasks if none of the characters are up to it.

- If they watch the wagons being unloaded, they'll notice Bog Luck directing laborers to carry the crates brought from the Greenfields into the warehouse. If they have a chance to see what's going on in the warehouse, they see that all the crates go into the strong room. If they don't look inside the warehouse while the wagons are unloaded but inspect the warehouse later, they won't find any of the crates; the only other place they could have gone is into the strong room.

- Gristle Pete, who sleeps above the strong room, hears strange noises on certain nights. He mistakes those noises for rats, but they come from lizardfolk carrying contraband into the tunnel beneath the strong room.
- They can take the direct approach and inspect the strong room surreptitiously. This leads to a fight with lizardfolk if characters search the room in the dead of night. Getting in by picking the lock is the safest approach. Trying to lift the key from Bog Luck's belt can work, but it's risky. If he catches someone in the attempt, a beating is the best they can hope for. A smart character submits to this humiliation, because fighting back means that Bog Luck calls everyone else to help him punish the thief, and all the characters are ostracized from then on. Taking the beating means Bog Luck keeps the incident between the two of them.
- Characters can arrange to have a room next to the Cult of the Dragon teamsters and listen through the walls to the cultists' conversation. They can't make out entire conversations, but they do pick out the words "strong room," "tunnel," "lizardfolk," and "Bog Luck."
- Talking to other escorts and wagon drivers yields some interesting observations but no concrete leads. Most of the others who came along on the haul north of Waterdeep agree that there's something standoffish about the cultists (they don't use that word).
- Searching the cultists' two rooms turns up something a personal bag containing six polished gems and small, easily concealed items of jewelry, all together worth about 1,400 gp. The cultists have a thief among them: a half-elf named Larion Keenblade. If he can be identified and accosted away from the others, he might agree to help the characters in exchange for their help getting away.

Grudge Match

A friend of the cultist murdered by Jamna has nurtured a grudge against a character since that incident. Now that their load is safely delivered and the mission is complete, this cultist can seek vengeance for her slain friend.

At an opportune time, the cultist tries to goad the character into a fight. She'll use any incident she can from their time together, including the murder, to question the character's courage and fighting ability in front of everyone. If the character refuses to bite, the cultist doesn't back down. The NPC wants blood and won't settle for anything less. She draws her sword and attacks. The cultist uses the stats of a **veteran**.

As far as the other cultists, teamsters, and hired guards are concerned, this is a personal issue between these two. If the character backs down, everyone assumes the character is a coward and treats this character with disrespect for the rest of his or her time at the camp. If other characters jump into the fight at their companion's side, more cultists do the same (treat them as twelve **guards**). Bog Luck and Ardred Briferhew prevent anyone else from joining in, but they don't mind watching some limited bloodshed to break the boredom.

The cultist means to kill the character, and she will if she wins the duel (continuing to stab the body after the character is at 0 hit points) and no one stops her.

EPISODE 6: CASTLE NAERYTAR

The tunnel from the roadhouse emerges in a spot nearby that's screened by trees and brush from the camp. As characters approach through the tunnel, any of them with a passive Wisdom (Perception) score of 10 or higher hears bestial voices ahead, growling and murmuring indistinctly in Draconic. From there, a trail leads into the Mere of Dead Men, where a mix of swamp denizens and cultists of the dragon vie for power at the ruins of Castle Naerytar.

This stout, stone castle was the home of a half-elf wizard, but he abandoned it long ago when the swamp claimed the area. For a time, a group of astrologers called the Academy of Stargazers took over the structure, but they vanished mysteriously after a few years. No one knows what became of them. Before the group's destruction, the members modified the castle by building an observatory into the top floor of the keep. Some of their magical viewing equipment is still there.

Now the Cult of the Dragon has moved people into Castle Naerytar and formed shaky alliances with nearby swamp dwellers, but the surrounding swampland is far from under anyone's control. The cult brought lizardfolk, bullywugs, and a pair of black dragons together in an unstable alliance, but the factions are riven by deep distrust that outsiders can exploit.

TRAVELING TO THE CASTLE

Castle Naerytar is not just a stone's throw down the road. It sits fifteen miles from the work camp—fifteen cold, muddy, difficult miles. It takes the characters two days to cover that ground at a moderate pace. Fortunately, the trail is marked by the lizardfolk who transport contraband through the mere to Castle Naerytar for the cult. Without the trail, finding the castle in this snarled, confusing maze would depend more on luck than skill. This trail doesn't make travel easy; the lizardfolk's trail is still treated as difficult terrain. It only shows the direction to go.

Day 1. The first day's travel is by foot through tangled marsh. The ground is what passes for dry in the mere: even "solid ground" is soggy, with water very near the surface. Lizardfolk porters carry the cult's contraband on their backs along this portion of the trail, and their tracks can be plainly seen where the path crosses wet ground. Much of the path is through mucky, cold, knee-deep water. On those stretches, blaze marks are cut into trees to keep porters on the right course. No skill checks are needed to avoid getting lost as long as characters stick to the trail. If characters leave the trail, then a successful DC 15 Wisdom (Survival) check is needed to find it again. Each check equates to an hour of searching, which calls for a random encounters check.

Evening 1. After seven miles of progress, characters reach a campsite at the approximate halfway point on the trip between the work camp and Castle Naerytar.

> It isn't much of a camp—just a clearing that's slightly drier than the muck you've been wading through—but four wicker lean-tos and a stone platform (for lighting a fire above the soggy ground) command attention in this wilderness. Three dugout canoes are drawn up near one of the lean-tos.
>
> A few dozen yards beyond the campsite in the direction you've been traveling, dry land ends. Other than moss-covered trees, fallen logs, and thick clumps of reeds, nothing rises above the still, black water.

Each canoe has three paddles and is large enough to hold five humans without much gear, or two or three with packs and other gear. Inside the lean-tos are a few baskets containing smoked fish (edible) along with some lizards and birds that have been smashed flat and dried in the sun (very unappetizing to humans but edible).

If characters arrive before dusk, the camp is empty and they can explore it safely. No random encounters bother characters while they're in the campsite. As the sun begins to set, nine **lizardfolk** paddle up in three canoes. They are traveling from Castle Naerytar to the roadhouse to pick up a load of contraband. The lizardfolk expect no trouble near their camp, so if characters posted a watch, then those characters who are actively on watch notice the approaching lizardfolk automatically and the lizardfolk are surprised. If characters lit a fire, however, then the lizardfolk smell the smoke from quite a distance away and know someone is in the camp. They assume it's more of their own kind returning from the work camp with treasure bound for Castle Naerytar, but the mere is filled with potential enemies and one never knows for sure, so their approach is more cautious if they smell smoke. In that case, characters with passive Wisdom (Perception) scores of 10 or higher notice the approaching lizardfolk canoes before the lizardfolk spot the strangers in their camp.

These lizardfolk won't negotiate or converse with characters. They've been told by the elf who commands operations at Castle Naerytar that strangers in the mere are to be killed or captured but never engaged in conversation. If they are captured and tied up, a successful DC 10 Charisma (Intimidation) or DC 15 Charisma (Persuasion) check loosens their tongues. If the lizardfolk aren't tied up, characters have disadvantage on these rolls because the lizardfolk think them soft-hearted.

Lizardfolk know that they're transporting treasure to the castle. The "dragon kneelers" take it into the castle, and the lizardfolk never see it again. They are paid in steel blades (they have no ability to manufacture with metal) and magic talismans. All the lizardfolk wear necklaces and bracelets made of bone, teeth, feathers, carved soft stone, and leather. On close inspection, characters see mixed in among these things traces of civilization: glass beads, coins, costume jewelry, tiny mirrors, and stamped copper and tin amulets of the sort that can be bought for a few pennies at any trinket shop or souvenir stand. None of it is magical.

During the questioning, have every character make a Charisma check. Whichever character scores highest makes a strong impression on a lizardfolk captive. This lizardfolk, whose name is Snapjaw, is unhappy about the situation in the mere, and he develops the notion that these strangers could be the key to driving out the cultists and to slaughtering their cruel bullywug allies. Snapjaw tries to communicate with the chosen character, but he doesn't want any of his comrades to know. He speaks enough pidgin Common to converse in simple terms, in case no one in the party speaks Draconic.

How Snapjaw goes about opening a dialog depends on the situation. If he's the only surviving lizardfolk or he's questioned out of earshot from the others, he can speak openly. If several lizardfolk are tied up and they're being questioned together, he could sprinkle words of Common into his Draconic replies, such as "want to help" and "talk alone." If several lizardfolk are tied up and left alone for a few minutes, he could scratch a similar message into the ground. He might try provoking a character into a wrestling match or a duel (if your players are the type to take up such a challenge), and then whisper his message into the character's ear.

If characters don't mistreat Snapjaw and don't kill any more lizardfolk than they need to, he becomes a reliable ally for as long as they work against the cult and the bullywugs. Roll a die for each of the other lizardfolk captives. On an even roll, Snapjaw persuades that lizardfolk to join his little revolt. On an odd roll, that NPC refuses to cooperate under any circumstance.

Day 2. From the campsite on, the trip to Castle Naerytar must be made by canoe. Snapjaw can guide the characters. A guide isn't really necessary, because the course is marked with symbols scratched into tree trunks and totems hung from branches.

MERE OF DEAD MEN RANDOM ENCOUNTERS

The Mere of Dead Men is a place filled with dangerous creatures. Roll a d20 per hour of travel; an encounter occurs on a roll of 18–20. Determine the encounter by rolling on the table below, or choose an encounter.

MERE OF DEAD MEN ENCOUNTERS

d12	Encounter
1–2	Bullywugs (2 or 3 per character)
3	Crocodiles (2 per character)
4	Giant frogs (2 per character)
5	Giant lizards (2 per character)
6	Giant spiders (1 per character)
7–8	Lizardfolk (3 per 2 characters)
9	Quicksand
10	Shambling mound
11	Will-o'-wisps (3)
12	Yuan-ti hunting party (see below)

Bullywugs. Bullywugs patrol the mere haphazardly. Before characters reach the midway campsite, this encounter is with two bullywugs per character. After characters reach the midway campsite, this encounter is with three bullywugs per character. Not all bullywugs in the mere work for the cult, but any the characters run into do.

Crocodiles. An encounter with crocodiles always occurs in water at least 2 feet deep. The first time characters run into crocodiles in the mere, the creatures have advantage on their Stealth check.

Giant Frogs. Giant frogs use their sticky tongue attacks whenever they can, and they prefer halflings, gnomes, and other small targets over creatures they can't swallow.

Giant Lizards. Giant lizards of the Mere of Dead Men have the Hold Breath trait. There is a 30 percent chance that these are trained lizards moving ahead of a lizardfolk encounter group. If so, those lizardfolk (see below) appear on the scene at the start of the sixth round of combat.

Giant Spiders. The spiders' web is nearly invisible in an area of heavy fog. Spiders of the Mere of Dead Men have the Hold Breath trait.

Lizardfolk. The lizardfolk of the mere are reluctant allies of the cult, mostly because Dralmorrer Borngray allows the more numerous bullywugs to push them around. The odds are 50 percent whether a group of lizardfolk works for the cult or is independent. An independent group helps the characters if Snapjaw is present to persuade them. They won't tackle the cult or a large group of bullywugs head-on, but they can help by scouting and creating diversions. Lizardfolk that do work for the cult attack immediately if they see Snapjaw tied like a prisoner. If Snapjaw is loose and characters don't seem hostile toward him, the lizardfolk hesitate, wondering whether the characters are cultists themselves.

Quicksand. A creature that steps into the quicksand must succeed on a DC 11 Dexterity saving throw or sink into the quicksand and be restrained. On its turn, as part of its movement, the trapped creature can escape by making a DC 15 Strength check. Another creature can attempt to pull the restrained creature out of the quicksand as an action but must succeed on a DC 15 Strength check to do so. As in a movie, the trapped creature is always more than 5 feet from the edge of the quicksand, so rescuers can't just grab the character; they must find a vine, a rope, or a pole and toss it to where the trapped character can reach it.

Shambling Mound. All the lizardfolk, Snapjaw included, are terrified of "the weed that walks." If it appears while Snapjaw is with the characters, he spends 1 round urging the characters to flee, then does so himself. Unless someone follows him immediately, it will take an hour to find him again.

Will-o'-Wisps. If this encounter occurs before characters reach the midway camp, the wisps don't show themselves immediately but instead follow the characters invisibly until nightfall. Then they try to lure just one or two characters into following them, by appearing as indistinct, flickering lanterns passing nearby. Anyone who follows the lights even a short distance is lured into a patch of quicksand. If the encounter occurs after characters leave the midway camp, then the will-o'-wisps use the same trick but in heavy morning fog, and instead of luring characters into quicksand, they lure them to the lair of Voaraghamanthar, the black dragon.

Yuan-ti Hunting Party. All residents of the mere, including the lizardfolk, the cultists, and especially the bullywugs, fear and despise the yuan-ti. For their part, the yuan-ti despise everyone right back, but they have no fear. This group of two **yuan-ti malisons** (type 1) and three **yuan-ti purebloods** is hunting for any intelligent creatures that would be suitable sacrifices to their long-slumbering god Merrshaulk. Yuan-ti won't ally with anyone or against anyone.

CASTLE NAERYTAR

Over a century ago, a half-elf wizard built a castle at the edge of the Mere of Dead Men. He lived there a relatively short time before the growing swamp flowed past the castle on all sides and made the location too remote for even his taste. After the structure sat abandoned for years, a group of astrologers called the Academy of Stargazers claimed it. They built an observatory into the top level of the keep, where they installed a piece of magic equipment called the *farseer of Illusk*. But the astrologers vanished mysteriously after a few years.

After the disappearance of the astrologers, the castle again fell into disuse. It was built to withstand its cold, watery environment, so the encroaching water hasn't undermined the walls or flooded the dungeon. Over decades of abandonment, however, it filled with debris and attracted many unpleasant dwellers. Then Rezmir happened upon the castle on one of her trips into the mere to study and negotiate with the black dragon Voaraghamanthar. Rezmir suspected the castle could become a useful stronghold for her, being located so conveniently close to the lair of a black dragon. She explored the structure, cleared the giant spiders out of the tower, and forged an alliance with the nearby tribe of bullywugs.

During that time, the half-dragon was still thinking of the castle simply as a fortified hideout. When she discovered the portal in the dungeon and learned that it connected to an abandoned lodge in the Graypeak Mountains, a new thought took shape. Lugging large amounts of treasure fifteen miles through the mere would not be easy, but if it cut 700 miles of wagon transport out of the picture, it would be worth the difficulty—especially if bullywugs and lizardfolk did all the hard work. Rezmir laid claim to both structures, turned the Graypeak Mountain hunting lodge over to a trusted Cult of the Dragon associate (a half-elf named Talis who now despises Rezmir—see episode 7), and set about making Castle Naerytar an essential hub in the cult's treasure-amassing activity in the North.

Through diplomacy and intimidation, and by leveraging the influence of Voaraghamanthar with the monstrous creatures of the mere, Rezmir created an uneasy alliance in the Mere of Dead Men and brought her vision into reality.

FACTIONS

Three power groups operate around Castle Naerytar: the Cult of the Dragon, a band of bullywugs, and a lizardfolk tribe. The black dragon Voaraghamanthar, along with its kobold and lizardfolk minions, could constitute a fourth group if it took an active hand in events, but for now it is biding its time to see how events develop.

Rezmir's three-way alliance is unstable. The cultists despise living in the swamp and have little respect for the bullywugs or lizardfolk; the leader of the bullywugs would like to seize Castle Naerytar for his own purposes; the bullywugs in general take every opportunity to push around the lizardfolk; and the lizardfolk chafe under the abuse of the bullywugs and wonder why Voaraghamanthar doesn't step in to protect them.

CULT OF THE DRAGON

Although Rezmir is responsible for resurrecting Castle Naerytar and claiming it for the Cult of the Dragon (in name only; she considers it her personal property), an elf Wearer of Purple named **Dralmorrer Borngray** (see appendix B) commands the castle for Rezmir. The half-dragon needs to show up occasionally to remind the bullywugs and lizardfolk that the Cult of the Dragon is really in charge, but Borngray runs the operation.

Dralmorrer Borngray is a member of the Eldreth Valuuthra, a group of elf supremacists dedicated to removing humanity from Faerûn. He longs for the age of great empires before humans claimed the continent. Being from Evermeet, he believes that his island home will be safely sheltered from the dragons' reign. Elves on the mainland will suffer, but that will be a small price to pay for the terror that will fall on humanity.

The elf idolizes Rezmir in all ways but one: he rues her decision to elevate the bullywugs in their alliance. In Borngray's opinion, the lizardfolk would be more useful, more reliable, and more appropriate allies than the repulsive bullywugs are. He cannot alter the arrangement without countering Rezmir's orders, but Borngray has taken small steps to restore the lizardfolk's tribal pride, such as by trying to teach them metallurgy. His effort has met with little success.

Borngray is loyal to the cult and yearns for Tiamat's return. He genuinely looks forward to the whole world lying helpless under the claws of dragons, both because that's where the world belongs, and because it will mean that his job at Castle Naerytar is finished. The second-best day of his life will be the day when Borngray can scrape the mud and stink of the Mere of Dead Men off his boots and return to someplace civilized. He has never mentioned his desire to leave to the bullywugs, whom he considers revolting necessities.

Only a handful of true Cult of the Dragon initiates and officers resides at the castle. All of them are noted in the castle description. They act as overseers and aides to Borngray and Rezmir.

BULLYWUGS

The band of bullywugs serving the Cult of the Dragon follows the dictates of **Pharblex Spattergoo** (see appendix B), a rare bullywug who has mastered shamanistic magic. His "religion" is a mishmash of confused tradition, borrowed mysticism, hallucinogenic intoxicants, and manufactured lore that serves more as a road to personal power for Pharblex than as a spiritual system for the bullywugs. Pharblex's spellcasting holds his followers together, and that makes him useful to Rezmir.

Pharblex hopes that when Tiamat returns, Rezmir will hand Castle Naerytar over to him, and he will rule the entire Mere of Dead Men from the castle. The only obstacle he sees between himself and his goal is the castle's current master, Dralmorrer Borngray; the notion that someone might want to not live in a swamp

PHARBLEX SPATTERGOO

has never entered Pharblex's narrow mind, and the bullywug seems deaf to Borngray's ironic and sarcastic jabs at the mere. When the time is right, Pharblex plans to remove the elf from the picture by any means necessary. It is unlikely that he would choose the middle of a battle against the characters, when he and Borngray are fighting side by side, to betray the elf—but it's not impossible. If it looks like the cult's operation at the castle is doomed, Pharblex is the sort of creature who will switch sides to save his slimy skin. The timing must be perfect, because he fears Rezmir more than he fears the characters. If, however, the characters have won the lizardfolk over to their side, slaughtered or driven off most of the bullywugs, overrun the castle, and are poised to kill Borngray and Pharblex in battle—Pharblex judges that the ideal time to forsake old allies and court new ones has arrived. He offers just about anything in exchange for the characters leaving him alive and in possession of Castle Naerytar (with or without the *farseer of Illusk* in operating condition).

The number of bullywugs around the castle fluctuates. They come and go as they please. On any given day, forty to fifty are camped outside the castle. Thirty-four more plus Pharblex live in the castle barracks (areas 1G and 2G). Another thirty to seventy are in the immediate area, close enough to respond within fifteen minutes to the beating of the drum in the barbican.

The bullywugs already believe themselves to be lords of the mere, and they act like it. They are easily confused, however. Under normal circumstances, they attack adventurers on sight, provided the bullywugs had superior numbers. They have grown accustomed to seeing cultists of many races coming and going around the castle, so when they see strangers, their first assumption is that the newcomers are more cultists. This assumption is reinforced if Snapjaw or other lizardfolk accompany the strangers or if the characters have any overtly cultish gear or clothing.

This doesn't mean characters can wander at will through the camp and the castle. Bullywug guards still challenge them to ask who they are and where they're going (in fractured pidgin Common if none of the characters speak Bullywug). They just don't assume that every stranger is an enemy and attack on sight.

Lizardfolk

The Scaly Death lizardfolk tribe has no leader. Pharblex killed its shaman, Suncaller, and the death left the tribe with an inferiority complex that was ripe for exploitation. When Rezmir promised that Voaraghamanthar would reward the tribe's labors for the cult, the lizardfolk were ready to listen.

Where the bullywugs fill the role of a static defense force, the lizardfolk perform five functions. First, they are the cult's laborers and porters. Lizardfolk did most of the heavy work while clearing debris from the castle, and they carry most of the treasure from the work camp to the castle on their backs and in their canoes. Second, they tend the giant lizards that are used to drag or carry especially heavy loads through the mere. Third, they do most of the hunting, fishing, and gathering to feed everyone at the castle. Fourth, they act as the castle's far-ranging scouts and outlying guards, since they are far superior to any bullywug at actively patrolling, ambushing, and laying traps. Fifth, a cadre of lizardfolk has been enlisted as elite guards for the castle itself. Borngray doesn't expect that any force would ever mount a real attack against the castle; it's too inaccessible, lying deep in the swamp. But if that unlikely event ever happened, he knows that the swaggering bullywugs would desert rather than fight an organized enemy. The lizardfolk, on the other hand, can be courageous and disciplined when they have a leader worth following. Borngray hopes to be that leader, at least to the small contingent of lizardfolk warriors he houses in the castle and rewards with special treatment. In exchange for their work, Borngray "pays" the tribe in metal weapons that are brought to the castle along with the loot.

Meanwhile, the bullywugs boss and bully the lizardfolk, emboldened by their superior numbers, the lizardfolk's instinctive awe of Pharblex's magic, and the absence of any restraining sign from Borngray or from the lair of the black dragon. Voaraghamanthar's silence, more than anything else, makes the lizardfolk wonder whether fate is punishing them for some unknown transgression. They grumble, and occasionally a few desert, but most of them bear up with reptilian stoicism.

Snapjaw is one of the few who has suggested rebelling against the hated bullywugs and the cultists. He hasn't done so openly, because that would invite retribution from the bullywugs, but he has spoken to a few fellow tribesfolk he trusts. Their response was interested but noncommittal; they intend to take revenge on the bullywugs, but not until the omens are right. Meanwhile, they endure—and stockpile weapons. Borngray has only a rough idea of how many lizardfolk are in the tribe all together, and he hasn't kept close count over how many swords, spears, daggers, shields, and metal-tipped arrows have been turned over to them. The lizardfolk are much better armed at this point than they let on to either the bullywugs or the cultists. When the time comes to move against the bullywugs, the lizardfolk intend for every bullywug throat and belly to be slit open with a new, razor-sharp steel blade.

Like the bullywugs, the lizardfolk's first assumption on seeing strangers is that they are cultists, or allies of the cultists, come to work or parley at the castle. They don't share the bullywugs' arrogance, however, so unless they are attacked, they don't really care who wanders through the camp. Lizardfolk on patrol or standing guard are an exception. They are alert, and they assume everyone is a potential enemy. They won't attack until they know for sure, lest they incur the wrath of Rezmir or Borngray for killing an ally. As outlying guards, their instructions are to alert the camp when strangers approach, keep the strangers under observation, and await further instructions.

The Scaly Death tribe comprises eighty lizardfolk warriors, both male and female. About half of them are in the vicinity of the castle at any given time; twenty-six live in the castle and the rest in reed huts (area 3). The others are away hunting, fishing, patrolling, hauling contraband from the work camp, or visiting their families in the tribal village (a few hours away to the southwest).

RED WIZARDS

Only one Red Wizard is present at Castle Naerytar: Azbara Jos, who was also in the cult camp on the Greenfields and traveled north with Rezmir. He has no interest in the Mere of Dead Men, bullywugs, or lizardfolk, and just slightly more interest in black dragons. He is here only as Rath Modar's liaison to Rezmir. The portal beneath the castle piques Jos's interest, however; portals are always of concern to the Red Wizards.

Adventurers appearing at this remote, secret site also interest him. If Azbara Jos sees the characters or learns of their presence, he arranges a private meeting—one that Rezmir and Borngray don't even know about, let alone attend. He wants to learn how much the characters know of the cult's plans, where and how they uncovered the information, who else knows about it, and what they think of the plan's chance to succeed. If the characters are captured and locked up in the castle, Jos finds an opportunity to ask all the same questions, again privately, but he is in a better position to force answers out of the characters.

This assumes the characters are at Castle Naerytar posing as cultists or hiding among the lizardfolk. If they're rampaging through the castle, killing everyone they meet, then Azbara Jos has only one concern: escaping through the portal before someone or something kills him.

VOARAGHAMANTHAR

Voaraghamanthar is an adult black dragon who claims the Mere of Dead Men as his territory. Although many creatures live in the mere and dominate it to one extent or another, none challenge Voaraghamanthar's supremacy. The bullywugs consider him a constant threat and tremble whenever his shadow passes near. The yuan-ti grant him grudging respect and covet his immense wealth. The lizardfolk honor him and wonder why he allows the cultists to abuse them. The cultists venerate him and divert some of the arriving contraband to his lair as tribute.

Voaraghamanthar has a secret that is known to only two other creatures in Faerûn. One of them is Rezmir. The other creature *is* the secret: Waervaerendor, the twin brother of Voaraghamanthar. For centuries, these twins have misled the world into believing that only one dragon dwells in the Mere of Dead Men—one dragon that must travel at immense speed, since it has been spotted at widely separated locales in rapid succession. The siblings seldom leave their lairs, but when they do, they coordinate so they are never seen together or seen in two distant places at precisely the same time.

Rezmir persuaded the twins to pledge their aid to the cult, but so far, the pledge hasn't carried much weight. Neither dragon leaves its lair frequently enough to provide much help. Like all black dragons, these two are paranoid about all other dragons. Tiamat's potential return and the establishment of a vast dragon empire seem like remote possibilities compared to the real danger of tangling with another dragon, any of whom would gladly murder Voaraghamanthar and Waervaerendor for their hoards. That's the twins' outlook, anyway. While their concern over the murderous nature of other dragons is justified, the fact that they are two means they have little to fear from most solitary dragons. Rezmir is working hard to persuade them that they could gain great power by revealing their secret at the strategically correct moment. Until Tiamat's return looks more certain, however, Voaraghamanthar and Waervaerendor intend to keep playing it safe, stick close to home, and guard their secret.

Voaraghamanthar and Waervaerendor are not a true faction in the mere because they are not advancing any agenda of their own, but their presence affects the balance of power. Without Voaraghamanthar, the cult wouldn't be here at all. Without Voaraghamanthar, the lizardfolk probably could not have been maneuvered into making common cause with the bullywugs.

Characters should not encounter either of these dragons face to face in this adventure (they are likely to meet in *The Rise of Tiamat*). If characters stray from the lizardfolk's path between the work camp and Castle Naerytar, intentionally or unintentionally—if, for example, they follow will-o'-wisps into the mere—they could enter the blighted territory around one of the lairs. Many clues can inform characters that they're in dragon territory. First, they pass markers consisting of the acid-eaten skulls of humans, humanoids, yuan-ti, crocodiles, and just about every other creature that lives in the mere. The skulls hang from withered trees and from spikes driven into the ground.

Both dragons' lairs are heavily guarded by lizardfolk. The dragons' guards are selected from the Scaly Death lizardfolk that work for the cult. Kobolds infest the actual lairs, but they seldom come out into the mere.

SQUARING OFF AGAINST THE CULT OF THE DRAGON

Characters have several options at Castle Naerytar, and events there can go in many directions. Here are the key points to keep in mind when running this episode.

- Rezmir and Azbara Jos do almost anything to avoid a battle with interfering adventurers. They have bigger concerns than the safety of Castle Naerytar and its occupants. If a battle develops, both of these characters head directly for the gate beneath the castle and teleport to Talis the White's hunting lodge (see episode 7). For purposes of this adventure, do everything you can to ensure that Rezmir and Jos survive this episode. It's not a catastrophe if they don't, but it's much better if they do.
- Dralmorrer Borngray and Pharblex Spattergoo have everything to lose if enemies of the cult overrun Castle Naerytar; a defeat would cost Borngray his hard-earned rank in the cult, and Spattergoo would lose the base from which he hopes to rule the mere after the cult is finished with the castle. They fight to the death to protect the castle (simultaneously buying time for Rezmir and Jos to escape). Despite their loathing for one another, they understand that they are much stronger together than apart. As soon as fighting breaks out, they join forces and cooperate.

- The best place for Borngray and Pharblex to make their stand depends on how the attack develops; you'll need to play that part by ear. Their best ploy against a determined assault may be a fighting retreat through the castle and down into the caverns, where the narrow passages and giant frogs work in their favor.
- The bullywugs are numerous but cowardly. They fight to protect Pharblex, but if he isn't immediately in sight—if Pharblex has retreated into the caverns while other bullywugs are fighting in the inner ward, for example—bullywugs who feel as if he has abandoned them are likely to leap away into the mere and never come back. If Pharblex is killed, most bullywugs desert immediately.
- The lizardfolk are brave, but they despise the bullywugs. If characters haven't recruited the lizardfolk to their side, then the lizardfolk fight well whenever they're alone. If bullywugs are nearby, lizardfolk pull back and let the bullywugs bear the brunt of combat and casualties. If the lizardfolk have been won over to fighting alongside the characters, then they hunt bullywugs through the castle and grounds and murder them mercilessly. If bullywugs flee into the swamp, lizardfolk chase them. They are half-hearted when facing cultists—not because they fear the cultists but because they don't hate them, and they have a harder time mentally turning against that alliance.
- The cultists are dedicated but not fanatics, and they are laborers, not soldiers. They fight bravely with Dralmorrer Borngray leading them. Without him, the cultists' attacks are uncoordinated and hesitant. Their situation becomes even worse if they are fighting against rebellious lizardfolk. In that case, without Borngray to egg them on, they are most likely to barricade themselves in the upper levels of the southwest tower or the library and try to ride out the slaughter.

APPROACHING CASTLE NAERYTAR

How characters approach Naerytar can set the tone for everything that happens at the castle.

Snapjaw knows where the lizardfolk pickets are posted about half a mile out from the castle. If he is with the characters, he can prevent them from blundering into a trap or an ambush. He talks to the **6 lizardfolk** guards if characters let him. What he tells them depends on the opinion he's formed about the characters.

- If Snapjaw isn't yet sure whether the characters are the saviors he hopes they are, he tells the guards that these are cultists coming to join those already in the castle. The guards accept that story without question and let everyone pass.
- If the heroes have established strong trust between themselves and Snapjaw, he tells the guards that the characters are great warriors come to destroy the Cult of the Dragon, and that now is the time to make their move against the bullywugs. You can either decide for yourself how the guards react to that, or make a DC 10 Charisma check for Snapjaw. If the check succeeds, the guards are persuaded. If the check fails, the

characters don't impress them. They won't take action against the bullywugs now, but they won't interfere with the characters, either. If the result is 5 or lower, these guards decide Snapjaw's talk of an uprising is dangerously rash, and they attack him.
- If the characters have done nothing to win Snapjaw's trust or they've treated him no better than bullywugs would have, then he tells the guards that the characters are nothing but trouble, and the lizardfolk attack.

If Snapjaw is not with the characters, they still have a chance to detect the guard outpost on their own. Characters with passive Wisdom (Perception) scores of 15 or higher catch whiffs of wood smoke. Also make a single Dexterity (Stealth) check for the lizardfolk guards, with advantage (they've had plenty of time to conceal themselves). Compare their result to the characters' passive Wisdom (Perception) scores to see whether any of the characters notice the lizardfolk in hiding.

If the lizardfolk go undetected, they send two fast swimmers ahead by a secondary route to alert bullywugs at the castle. Two more scouts follow the characters while the last two remain at their post and continue keeping watch.

OUTSIDE CASTLE NAERYTAR

Castle Naerytar was built on dry land, then a deep, dry moat was dug around it. When the mere expanded and surrounded the castle site, the moat flooded and overflowed. Now the whole site is swampy, and large pools of standing water dot the clearing. The castle was built on exposed bedrock, so its foundation is sound and mostly dry even a century after the flooding. Tangled brush and trees grow to within twenty feet of the walls on three sides of the castle. Only the front (southern) face is clear.

Bullywugs live in crowded, hastily made reed huts. The lizardfolk have sturdier, roomier reed longhouses.

1. LANDING

A half-dozen dugout canoes are pulled up onto land here. Three to five paddles lie in the bottom of each. Five of them are in good condition; the sixth has a rotten bottom, and the lizardfolk never use it. If characters grab canoes in a hurry, there is a 1-in-6 chance they get the rotten one. It starts leaking as soon as it's put in water, and it sinks after fifteen minutes.

2. ANIMAL STOCKADE

The lizardfolk keep their giant lizards penned here. The five-foot-high wall of the stockade is made from sturdy logs driven into the earth, spaced about six inches apart, and bound together with twisted fiber. The lizards can carry or drag loads that are too massive for the lizardfolk, such as large timbers or impressive crocodiles. They are also used to raise stone onto the castle battlements through ropes and pulleys—technology that never ceases to amaze the lizardfolk. There are 2d4 **giant lizards** in the pen at any given time. They are ill-tempered and attack anyone who comes within reach if their handlers aren't present to keep them under control. If set loose, they most likely romp away into the swamp. If the goal is to have the lizards rampage through the camp, someone needs to rile them up first. Poking them through the stockade wall with spears will do the trick.

3. LONGHOUSES

The lizardfolk warriors live in these longhouses.

> The longhouses are made from reeds bound into long, thick bundles and bent into upside-down, U-shaped ribs. The spaces between the ribs are latticed and thatched with more reeds. Each longhouse has a single, woven door in the center of one end wall. The construction technique used in the longhouses is ingenious.

The lizardfolk may be technologically backward, but they are masters of their environment. They show the same building talent in their traps and snares.

Inside, longhouses are roomy and well ventilated. The ground is covered with reed mats, and the interior is dry and airy. Gear hangs from pegs on the walls to keep it off the ground. Lizardfolk are especially careful with their new, steel weapons, which rust quickly when exposed to dampness. They fill small stone ovens with coals for heat. There are no open fireplaces; the danger from sparks is too great.

Each of these longhouses could house twenty-five lizardfolk comfortably, and more with some crowding. When Rezmir first negotiated with the lizardfolk, they intended to move the entire village here, and built accordingly. As more bullywugs also flocked to the castle and the real situation became apparent, the warriors instructed their families to stay behind. Thus, they have far more longhouse space at the castle than they need. Characters observing the area from hiding and judging solely from the longhouses would estimate conservatively that over a hundred lizardfolk live at the castle. They won't count anywhere near that many lizardfolk in the clearing. Snapjaw can explain the discrepancy, if he's around.

4. HUTS

The bullywugs live in huts, which are crudely built.

> A dozen or more huts are placed haphazardly on the boggy ground. Each is shaped like a slightly flattened dome. The doorways are open, but a low, short tunnel forces a creature to crawl into the hut. They are made of reeds woven through a lattice, with a generous layer of mud, grass, and dung smeared over the whole thing. Mud, swamp water, and muck slops between the huts and even flows in and out of the low, open doorways.

The interiors of the bullywugs' huts are the complete opposite of the lizardfolk's longhouses: wet, filthy, sloppily made, and reeking. The floors aren't just damp; they're churned into mud pits up to 2 feet deep, so the bullywugs can rest froglike in mud up to their eyeballs. They have no sense of privacy or personal space. At night, they crowd in atop one another until everyone is squeezed. Bullywugs aren't assigned to any particular huts. They sleep in whichever is most convenient when they grow tired, so it's common for some huts to be packed at night while others sit completely empty.

Eight **giant frogs** hop randomly among the huts or sit silently in the pools of standing water. These creatures were raised from tadpoles by the bullywugs and don't bother them, but they attack anyone else who carelessly wanders within reach of their 15-foot-long tongues.

5. MOAT

The muddy water lapping against the castle walls is indistinguishable at a glance from the puddles and hip-deep water standing throughout the area, but it hides a moat. Portions of the moat around the southwest tower have filled in to ground level, but elsewhere it is 30 to 40 feet wide and up to 15 feet deep. The causeway (1A) arches over the moat, providing a visual clue that the water may be deeper than it appears. Anyone splashing around in the moat attracts the attention of six **crocodiles**.

6. MAIN GATE

This is the only entrance into the castle that's used. When the castle was built, a pair of stout wooden gates and an iron portcullis closed off this 12-foot-wide, 10-foot-high gateway. The gates are never closed; they now sag on their hinges so badly that it's not worth the effort of levering them into place for any reason short of an imminent attack. The portcullis is rigged so it can be dropped with a hard yank on a lever (located on the upper level, area 2A), but since it was last tested, the mechanism has rusted to the point where the gate will drop only 3 feet, then jam in place.

INSIDE CASTLE NAERYTAR

The castle's exterior walls average 10 feet thick. Interior walls are also stone but only about 1 or 2 feet thick.

Most of the structures inside the castle are more than one story tall. In the descriptions, areas are identified by floor, then letter, so area 1L is on the ground floor, 2L the second floor, and so on. If an area doesn't have an entry for a floor, then it doesn't exist on that floor.

GROUND FLOOR

1A. BARBICAN

The barbican is the primary defensive position for the castle. It is guarded round-the-clock by ten **bullywugs** and **1d6 giant frogs**. Unless a fight or other disturbance has happened somewhere, these guards are at low alertness.

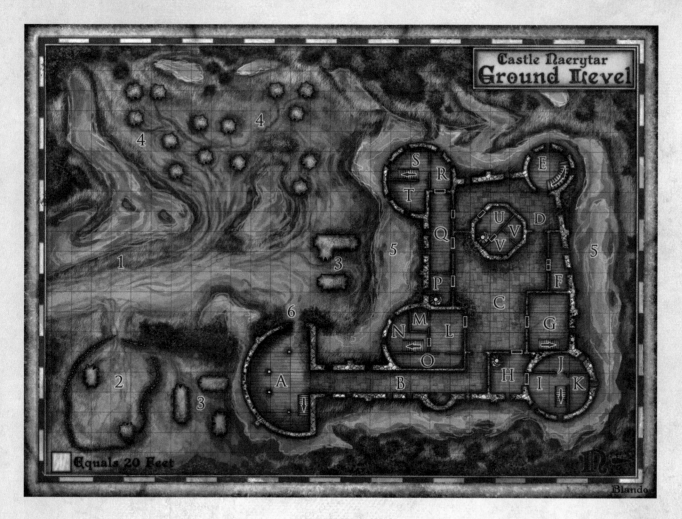

Castle Naerytar
Ground Level

Equals 20 Feet

Blando

Sloppy mud covers the stone floor of this large chamber. Planks have been laid from the gateway to the causeway entrance to create a 10-foot-wide raised boardwalk for the cultists, who don't enjoy walking through mud the way bullywugs do. The slippery mud makes everywhere off the planks difficult terrain for characters. A few tables have been thrown together from planks laid across barrels, with crudely made benches for seats. The tables and benches are nearly as muddy as the floor.

The barbican has no windows or arrow slits at ground level. During daytime, bright light is within 20 feet of the open gateway and the open doorway to the causeway. Everywhere else, oil lamps cast only dim light (because the bullywugs never clean them).

Stairs lead up to area 2A.

1B. Causeway

This 180-foot causeway crosses the moat and leads to the castle's outer ward. It has no roof so defenders on the upper floor of the barbican (area 2A) can launch arrows into attackers crowded onto the causeway. A small defensive bulge along the east wall of the causeway is never manned.

1C. Outer Ward

The ground here was once hard-packed earth, but the area in front of the barracks (area 1G) has been churned into mud by flapping bullywug feet. At any particular time, there are 1d6 – 1 **bullywugs** and 1d6 – 1 **lizardfolk** present in the outer ward. Lizardfolk are likely to be working (training their giant lizards), while bullywugs might be loafing or giving orders to the lizardfolk.

1D. Inner Ward

Originally, the passage between the outer and inner wards could be closed off with heavy wooden gates, but they have long since fallen apart and haven't been replaced. The inner ward is patrolled by three **guard drakes** at all hours of the day. They attack anyone they don't recognize or who isn't accompanied by someone they recognize.

1E. Northwest Tower

The door to this tower has been torn off its hinges and lies on the ground. Originally, a wooden floor was at ground level with a pit beneath it for confining prisoners. The wooden floor is completely rotted away, and the pit has been filled nearly to ground level with garbage and mud.

There must have been a wooden floor in this tower when it was built, to cover the dungeon pit beneath it. Now the floor is gone and the dungeon has been turned into a garbage pit and latrine filled with foul-smelling waste and swamp water to just a few feet below the level of the doorway. The floor above is badly rotted and large portions have collapsed. Through the gaping holes in the second floor, you can see that the third floor is still in good condition. But to reach the stone stairs that circle upward around the outer wall, you must cross 10 feet of indescribable muck.

The pit is home to an **otyugh** that consumes much of the castle's garbage. When characters arrive, it is sitting quietly submerged in the muck, making it undetectable unless characters stir the foul-smelling stuff with poles. If someone steps into the muck or leaps to the steps, the otyugh lashes out with its tentacles. A grappled character is dragged into the pit where, along with all the hazards of being savaged by an otyugh, there is the added danger of drowning. It's safe to assume that characters entering this tower will take a big gulp of clean air first, but the otyugh's attack might knock the wind out of them. Allow the attacked character to make a Constitution saving throw with a DC equal to 5 plus the damage caused by the otyugh's tentacle attack. A successful saving throw means the character has a lungful of air when dragged into the muck and can hold his or her breath for a number of minutes equal to 1 + his or her Constitution modifier, with a minimum of 30 seconds (5 rounds). Failure means the character's lungs are empty, and the character falls unconscious at the end of his or her turn after a number of rounds equal to the character's Constitution modifier unless the character breaks free from the otyugh's grasp before then. See the suffocating rules in the *Player's Handbook*.

1F. STABLES

The fittest, most ferocious of the giant lizards are housed here instead of in the open stockade (area 2), to protect them against the biting and clawing that goes on in the common enclosure. These lizards are used as riding mounts by lizardfolk on long patrols. The stalls, originally built for horses, have been enlarged to accommodate the beasts (eight **giant lizards**). The normally lethargic creatures grow agitated when strangers enter the stables. If characters linger for more than a minute, two of the lizards start lashing the walls with their tails. The others pick up the ruckus in short order so that within two minutes, all are thrashing at the walls and bellowing. The commotion draws four **lizardfolk** who are the giant lizards' handlers. The lizardfolk have a calming influence on the giant lizards, but if they are interfered with, the disquieted lizards smash through their stalls and attack anything in the stables.

A ladder in the southeast corner of the stables grants access to a loft above the stables.

1G. LOWER BARRACKS

This large structure was built to house the castle's garrison. Pharblex and his hand-picked circle of bullywug toughs has taken it over. Pharblex is seldom here, but during the day, twelve **bullywugs** lounge in the squalor. That number doubles at night.

If characters walk into the barracks during daytime, read the text below aloud. If they sneak in or enter in the middle of the night, adjust and paraphrase accordingly.

Twelve bullywugs eye you suspiciously from a room that might have been a tidy barracks once. Now it is largely empty of furniture, much of the floor is churned into mud, and the stink of bullywugs permeates everything.

If the bullywugs assume the characters are cultists, they tolerate their presence here on the lowest floor of the barracks. They won't allow anyone upstairs, and they won't take orders from someone they don't know and recognize. If a fight breaks out in this area, bullywugs from the upper level (area 2G) leap into the battle from the staircase on the third round.

Three mud-spattered chests are shoved into the sheltered space behind the staircase. These contain much of the bullywugs' accumulated pay. Dralmorrer Borngray pays them with articles of looted treasure that he deems too cheap or tacky to include in the hoard being accumulated for Tiamat. The chests contain hundreds of items made from copper and tin and that incorporate small or damaged semiprecious stones. The three chests combined contain 30,000 cp, 500 sp, and jewelry (copper and tin with ornamental or semiprecious stones) worth another 350 gp, for a total value of 700 gp. Their total weight is over 500 pounds: 305 pounds of coins plus another 200 pounds of jewelry.

Buried among all the copper and tin in one chest is a small mahogany box containing two *potions of healing* and one vial of *oil of etherealness*, overlooked by the cultists during sorting.

1H. FORGE AND ARMORY

Naerytar's builders set up this structure for the blacksmiths who would build and maintain the armor and weapons needed by the castle's defenders.

A large forge dominates the center of this chamber, which is pleasantly warm thanks to a bed of coals glowing dully in the forge. Half-a-dozen lizardfolk are working around the forge, but they don't seem to be accomplishing much. Other accouterments of the blacksmith's trade are scattered through the room, and many very poorly made metal items are heaped in the northwest corner.

A few months ago, Dralmorrer Borngray decided to put the forge back into operation. He despises Pharblex and the bullywugs, and he would prefer to deal solely with the lizardfolk if they could overcome the gloom that has gripped the tribe since Pharblex murdered their shaman. Borngray thought mastering a craft as advanced as metalworking would instill the lizardfolk with a renewed sense of pride. He might be right, but so far, the lizardfolk have shown little aptitude for the craft. They do, however, enjoy basking in the warmth of the forge, and they have learned to take excellent care of their new weapons even if they can't manufacture more.

The six **lizardfolk** in the forge room won't attack unless they are antagonized first. They are trying to make an iron spear point from scraps of ruined armor, but their effort is producing something more like a shovel than a blade. They listen attentively if characters offer advice but show no sign of comprehending what they're told.

1I. Lizardfolk Ready Room

The twenty **lizardfolk** selected by Dralmorrer Borngray to serve as his backup guards use this northeast tower as their barracks. This chamber is their daytime ready room. When they are not drilling with their weapons, the lizardfolk spend their time in this chamber, gambling, exercising, and telling stories of happier times. Borngray maintains this force as insurance against treachery by Pharblex and the bullywugs.

Like guards elsewhere in the castle, those in this room assume that strangers are newly arrived cultists unless they have reason to think otherwise (seeing strangers with weapons dripping blood from recent combat would be one such reason). They won't attack unless provoked, but they won't let anyone go upstairs or into areas 1J and 1K without an excellent reason, either.

1J. Lizardfolk Sleeping Room

The ten dominant lizardfolk guards rest in this chamber, because it gets more warmth from the forge (area 1H) than area 1K does. They sleep on reed pallets that are spread across the floor in no apparent pattern, and each keeps meager belongings beneath his "bed." Despite the lack of order, the room is clean and dry. It is empty during the day, but ten **lizardfolk** sleep here at night.

1K. Lizardfolk Sleeping Room

Ten lizardfolk guards sleep in this chamber. They are the less dominant half of Borngray's lizardfolk guards, consigned to this sleeping chamber because it gets less warmth from the forge (area 1H) than area 1J does. They sleep on reed pallets that are spread across the floor in no apparent pattern, and each keeps meager belongings beneath his "bed." Despite the lack of order, the room is clean and dry. It is empty during the day, but ten **lizardfolk** sleep here at night.

1L. Chapel

Over the years, this chapel has been consecrated to several different deities, depending on who ruled the castle. Now it is a shrine to Tiamat, adorned with a handsome wooden statue of the dragon queen crafted by lizardfolk. The workmanship is surprisingly good, though most of Tiamat's visages bear a stronger resemblance to lizardfolk than to dragons. A hidden compartment beneath Tiamat's black dragon head contains a *dagger of venom*. It can be found with a successful DC 15 Intelligence (Investigation) check. Only Rezmir and a few of the lizardfolk (including Snapjaw) who were involved in carving the statue know about the dagger.

The cultists venerate Tiamat but do not worship her, so the chapel is seldom used for anything that could be considered a religious observance or mass. Instead, individual cultists or small groups sometimes retire here for quiet reflection on how the world will suffer when the Queen of Dragons rises.

1M. Storeroom

All the trash from the chapel—broken stools, rotted altar cloths, corroded icons—was dumped in this room when the cultists took over. There's nothing of value here.

1N. Rectory

This was originally the castle priest's living quarters, and it included many sturdy storage cabinets for vestments and religious paraphernalia. All the cabinets were hacked open and looted long ago. Four **dragonclaws** (see appendix B) moved into this chamber and turned it into their living quarters. They tend the library in area 1N.

1O. Archer's Gallery

This long gallery overlooks the causeway through arrow slits. In case of an attack, archers could man it. The cultists don't use it for anything, and aside from cobwebs, it is empty.

1P. Kitchen

Meals for the cultists are prepared in this kitchen by a dwarf chef and his two human helpers (**commoners**). The chef is a **dwarf** named Tharm Tharmzid. If given the chance, he complains bitterly about the lack of ingredients here for good meals. Everything he receives comes from the lizardfolk hunters and gatherers, whose notions about what is and isn't edible don't mesh well with Tharmzid's.

1Q. Great Hall

The cultists eat their meals and conduct most of their business in this high, wide hall. The eastern end of the hall is used for dining and socializing. The western half is where contraband hauled in from the Carnath Roadhouse is inspected, cleaned, sorted, and repacked before being carried down to the portal beneath the southwest tower. The tables in that half of the hall are covered with valuables. The southwest corner of the room is a makeshift carpentry shop, where cultists build new chests and boxes to hold the plunder. If characters have a chance to paw through the piles and keep what they find, they get 450 gp, 520 sp, 80 pp, 22 semiprecious stones (5 × 35 gp, 6 × 45 gp, 6 × 55 gp, 4 × 65 gp, 1 × 80 gp), and a *potion of greater healing*. Alternatively, you can create your own expert-level hoard.

Looting won't be possible, however, as long as any cultists are alive. During the day, there will always be twelve **cultists** (of initiate rank) working in the Great Hall and four **dragonclaws** (see appendix B) keeping an eye on them. Most of the cultists are human, but all the character races are represented. The precise mix doesn't matter.

If there is any disturbance in the Great Hall, everyone within hearing responds to the hue and cry. Cultists in the southwest tower and guard drakes from the inner ward show up at the start of the third round, and any bullywugs or lizardfolk in the outer ward respond at the beginning of the fourth round.

At night, two **guard drakes** (see appendix B) sleep in the Great Hall while a third **guard drake** patrols the hall and the inner ward. Even asleep, the guard drakes are at normal alertness.

1R. Southwest Tower Antechamber

Swamp water seeps into this chamber through a crack in the foundation to pool inches deep on the sagging stone floor and fill the air with a cloying, moldy stink. The cultists laid a walkway of planks across the floor so they can walk between the two doorways without soaking their feet. This chamber isn't used for anything other than a passage between areas 1Q and 1R.

1S. Subterranean Entrance

The puddles in area 1R don't extend into this chamber, but the smell does. Because of that, the cultists use this chamber only as an accessway to other areas.

The most important feature of this chamber is the staircase that leads down to the caverns beneath the castle. It sits directly below the stairs that lead up to level two of the tower. There is no doorway across either set of steps. A door into area 1T is closed but not locked.

1T. Unused Chamber

This chamber is wet and moldy, though not flooded. The cultists don't use it because of the dampness, so giant centipedes have moved in and made a nest. Anyone who opens the door and enters the chamber becomes the target of ten **giant centipedes**.

If the characters pose as reinforcements sent by the cult, they are assigned this chamber as their quarters. Their first task is clearing out the centipedes, chinking leaks, and generally making the room livable.

1U. Keep Entrance

The entrance to the main keep is raised three steps above the level of the inner ward. A stout wooden door in good repair bars it, but the door is never locked or barred under normal circumstances.

This front chamber is a small version of the Great Hall, with a few tables and benches that are seldom used. Spiral stairs lead up to the second floor.

1V. West Guest Rooms

Normally, these rooms aren't used, but Azbara Jos occupies them currently. They are reasonably warm and comfortable. Jos will be here when he isn't consulting with Rezmir in area 1U, 2N, or 3L. Jos keeps all of his real valuables with him. The only things he leaves

in these chambers are his clothes and his traveling spellbook, which is locked inside a box of silver-inlaid redwood. The lock can be opened with a successful DC 15 Dexterity check, but if the roll is less than 20, the tampering sets off a magical ward with the same effect as a *Melf's acid arrow* spell; the acid arrow launches at the character who opened the box and causes 4d6 acid damage immediately plus another 4d6 acid damage at the end of the character's next turn. The damage is halved if the character makes a successful DC 15 Dexterity saving throw. Opening the box with the key disarms the trap automatically; Jos carries the key on a string around his neck.

Second Floor

2A. Upper Barbican

Although it is much cleaner than the lower level, the upper level of the barbican is still a mess. Muddy, webbed footprints of bullywugs trail up and down the stairs and fan out across the floor. This area is staffed by nine **bullywugs** day and night, but at night, they tend to sleep on watch.

This level of the barbican has no roof. Hundreds of melon-sized stones are piled around the battlements for throwing down on the heads of attackers. Many of the piles have collapsed, and the bullywugs are too lazy to restack them.

The causeway is fully exposed to archers positioned at the rear of the barbican, but the bullywugs seldom watch that direction.

The main feature of this area is a signal drum carved from an enormous hollow log. This drum can be heard for miles when it is beaten vigorously. The bullywugs send many different signals with the drum: they can recall patrols and foragers to the castle, wake up the camp, indicate mealtimes, announce changes of the guard, and sound a general alarm if the castle ever comes under attack. The drum is heard about six times on a typical day, and everyone who lives at the castle knows the meanings of the different drumbeats. Characters won't know what they mean without asking someone.

2E. Rotted Floor

The second level of the northwest tower is in bad shape. There are large holes where the floorboards have completely rotted away or fallen into the muck below, and the floorboards that remain are unlikely to support a human's weight. The beams are still strong, but they are slick with fungus and mold. A successful DC 10 Dexterity (Acrobatics) check is needed to cross the level on a beam without slipping and falling into the awfulness of area 1E.

Across the tower, up against the south wall, is a single, locked trunk. The lock can be opened with a set of thieves' tools and a successful DC 10 Dexterity check. The chest contains 1,825 cp, 54 sp, and a pair of garish gold earrings that would be worth another 10 gp if melted. The chest was left behind when the last tenants of the castle departed, being considered not worth the effort to lug down the stairs.

The stone steps that wind around the outer wall come

to a small (approximately 3 feet by 3 feet) stone landing, then continue upward to the third level. Characters are safe from falling as long as they stay on the landing or the steps.

A trapdoor closes off the top of the stairs at the ceiling. The door is latched with a simple wooden turn-button. The door also bears a warning but, because the warning was drawn in chalk nearly a century ago, it is all but invisible now. It can be noticed with a successful DC 20 Wisdom (Perception) check. After the chalk mark is noticed, anyone who reads Dwarvish can correctly interpret it as a warning that powerful undead reside in the room beyond. Adventurers placed the rune here decades ago after running afoul of the specters in area 3E.

2F. STABLES LOFT

The loft above the stables is where the lizardfolk store bundles of cut reeds to use as bedding in the stalls of the giant lizards. Other than reeds and a few bats, nothing else is here.

2G. UPPER BARRACKS

Pharblex Spattergoo (see appendix B) and his personal retinue of ten **bullywugs** use this level of the barracks as their living quarters. No one else has any business being in this chamber, including cultists. Not even Borngray or Rezmir herself are welcome here. The bullywugs are always here at night but only two stand guard over the treasure chest during the day, when Pharblex spends most of his time in the giant frog hatchery beneath the castle. Those two guards trust no one, and one of them is equipped with a horn made of crocodile bone with which to sound the alarm if trouble develops.

Like all areas occupied by bullywugs, this chamber is a mess. Reed pallets, dirty baskets, and animal bones litter the floor.

In the southeast corner of the room is a large, sturdy chest, wrapped in chains and padlocked. The lock can be picked with thieves' tools and a successful DC 12 Dexterity check. Inside is Pharblex's share of the bullywugs' pay: silver and electrum jewelry, hand mirrors, shell combs, hair pins and brooches with semiprecious stones, all with a total value of 1,376 gp. Most of the silver is black from tarnish. In a civilized land, every one of these items is something that would be found on a

woman's dressing table or nightstand. This is a private joke that Dralmorrer Borngray finds quietly hilarious. It's all the same to Pharblex, since he knows nothing of civilization or the fashions of human noblewomen.

2H. ARSENAL

This chamber was stocked with armor, weapons, and hundreds of arrows when the castle was abandoned. The metal rusted to dust, the arrows warped into uselessness, and the leather was chewed away by rats and other vermin. Now this chamber is the unofficial headquarters of the lizardfolk in the castle. Neither the bullywugs nor the cultists ever come up here.

The arsenal chamber is the warmest in the castle, thanks to heat rising from the forge (area 1H). The lizardfolk that live in the castle gather here—usually at night—to discuss their situation and what they should do. The debate is between accepting their fate as lowly servants of the Cult of the Dragon, attacking the bullywugs in a glorious yet suicidal assault, or biding their time until they can attack with a chance of winning.

The lizardfolk's stockpile of new weapons is hidden beneath stacks of rusted, rotten, century-old arms. Just a few minutes of searching through the junk can turn up one or two bundles of sharp, clean blades for shortswords, daggers, and spears, neatly wrapped in oilskin.

Unless the lizardfolk are meeting, this chamber usually is empty. The lizardfolk seldom come here when they could be observed gathering, to avoid attracting suspicion or making anyone curious about what's in the "unused" room above the forge.

2I, J, K. Vacant Rooms

Dralmorrer Borngray assigned the entire northeast tower to the lizardfolk for their use, but they sleep and live mainly on the ground floor. The second-floor rooms contain nothing of interest or value.

If characters poke around in this area, however, those with a passive Wisdom (Perception) score of 15 or higher notice that the doors between areas 2H, 2I, and 2K open and close smoothly and soundlessly, unlike most other doors in the castle, which squeak and squeal loudly on corroded hinges. The lizardfolk keep these doors well-oiled so they can slip up to area 2H in the dead of night without awakening any bullywugs in the barracks (areas 1G and 2G).

A trapdoor closes off the top of the stairs up to area 3I. The trapdoor isn't locked, but a pair of iron spikes has been hammered between the door and the frame. Opening the door requires either a DC 10 Strength check or ten minutes spent carefully prying out the spikes. If the door is forced and no one is standing by ready to catch the spikes, they clatter noisily down the steps.

If characters are captured, they are confined in area 2J.

2L. Outer Library

Dralmorrer Borngray has converted the second floor of the chapel into a library. This chamber at the top of the stairs contains a few crates and chests of books culled from the arriving treasure that haven't been sorted and cataloged yet. Otherwise, it is empty.

2M. Reading Room

A small table and two chairs are the only furnishings in this chamber.

2N. Library

Since treasure first started funneling through Naerytar, Dralmorrer Borngray has pulled out any books, parchments, tablets, and other written material that interested him. He knows better than to claim it as his own; he will forward these treasures to Tiamat's hoard when the work at Castle Naerytar draws to a close. Until then, he keeps the written material at the castle to study and to divert him from the miserable surroundings. Rezmir knows about the library and approves of using the books this way, as long as they are delivered to the Well of Dragons before Tiamat's arrival.

Borngray has assembled an impressive library. It contains over one hundred books, quartos, and manuscripts covering the history of the Sword Coast, natural philosophy, mathematics, astronomy, magic, and many theoretical works on alternate reality, time, and dimensional travel. This collection would be a priceless addition to any library or collector in Waterdeep if it could be removed from the castle before the cultists spirit it away or the bullywugs spoil it.

The books and manuscripts are stored on wooden shelves built by the cultists from salvaged lumber.

One **dragonwing** (see appendix B) and four **cultists** (initiates) spend most of their time here, organizing the books.

2P. Kitchen Storage

Items that are needed in the kitchen (area 1P) occasionally but not every day are stored here, along with nonperishable food such as cooking oil, grain, cheese, wine, and salted meat.

2R. Cultists' Sleeping Chamber

The lowest-ranking cultists sleep here. At night, five **cultists** are present. Otherwise, the chamber is empty of all but their reed mattresses and simple belongings in wooden trunks. A small stone hearth in area 2T provides meager warmth.

2T. Cultists' Sleeping Chamber

At night, seven **dragonwings** (see appendix B) sleep here. Otherwise, the chamber is empty of all but their reed mattresses and simple belongings in wooden trunks. A small stone hearth keeps the chamber warm.

2U. Dralmorrer Borngray's Common Room

The second level of the keep is occupied entirely by Dralmorrer Borngray. This chamber is a combination sitting room and office, and a small hearth along the western wall provides heat. A writing desk, a large padded chair, and a bench are drawn up near the hearth. Otherwise, the room is largely empty.

2V, W. Borngray's Sleeping and Dressing Rooms

Area 2V is Borngray's sleeping chamber, furnished with a bed, a carpet-draped table with a wash basin and grooming supplies (comb, brush, soap, scented waters), and a stool. Rugs cover most of the floor. A raven in a large cage squawks loudly enough to be heard in the outer ward if a stranger enters the chamber, and the squawking awakens and draws the cultists and dragonwings from areas 2R and 2T to the tower.

Borngray is seldom here except when sleeping, immediately before retiring, and immediately after rising.

In addition to the elf's clothing and personal effects, a small strongbox is hidden beneath a loose floorboard under a rug. The hiding place is spotted automatically if the rug is moved and missed automatically if the rug is left alone. The strongbox contains Borngray's emergency funds: 200 gp, 200 sp, and 10 precious stones worth 100 gp each. The locked box can be opened with a key from Borngray's belt or with a set of thieves' tools and a successful DC 15 Dexterity check.

Third Floor

Many of the topmost levels of the castle are unused by cultists. Some of them are still home to dangerous creatures that were sealed off instead of being cleared out.

3E. Specters' Sanctum

Several years after its builder and original owner abandoned Castle Naerytar, the castle was re-occupied by an all-female school of astrologers called the Academy of Stargazers. A few years after the astrologers moved in, they were wiped out by their own leader. Several of the castle's residents were murdered in this topmost room of the northwest tower in particularly hideous fashion. They are still here in the form of three **specters** haunting the chamber. They rest quietly, ignoring everything and everyone in the castle, until someone opens the trapdoor and enters.

The open chamber contains a large table and star charts in scroll racks around the walls. Three bodies are sprawled on the floor, reduced by time to powdery bones and dusty tatters of cloth. As soon as someone enters the room, they rise as specters and attack. They pursue anywhere in the castle, but they won't leave the castle. They attack other living creatures if they can't get at those who disturbed their rest, but they prefer the intruders over anyone else.

Most of the paper star charts crumble into dust when touched, but three are still sturdy enough to be carried away. One of these was drawn on parchment, one scribed on a clay disc, and one etched on thinly rolled copper. The surviving charts would fetch 700 gp each from an astrologer in Waterdeep or other major city.

3G. Unused Chamber

Originally, this level of the barracks was used for storage and for training during severe weather. Several fencing dummies and targets still stand around the room, but they will fall apart if put to hard use.

3H, I, J. Spiders' Lair

The top level of the northeast tower is the lair of five **giant spiders**. They hunt in the swamp at night and return to the tower to rest during the days, entering through a hole in the roof. The spiders are wary, so they've never been seen coming and going. The lizardfolk know of them but haven't mentioned them to others.

The chamber is not hung with webs, but the cracked and bones of many animals (including bullywugs) litter the floor. The spiders nestle among the deep shadows between ceiling beams, and they have advantage on Dexterity (Stealth) checks while hidden in their recesses.

A trapdoor is closed across the steps from area 2K and jammed shut with two iron spikes driven between the door and the frame. See the description of area 2K for notes about opening the door. The door is sufficient to keep the spiders out of the lower levels of the tower, since the spiders and the lizardfolk have an unspoken understanding to leave each other alone. That doesn't extend to strangers such as the characters.

3L. Rezmir's Office

The third floor of the old chapel is converted to living quarters for Wyrmspeaker Rezmir. No one else uses these chambers even when Rezmir is away from the castle for tendays or months at a stretch.

The furnishings in all four chambers are lavish—surprisingly so, compared to everything else at the castle. All other furnishings were built on site, but Rezmir's come from the workshops of the finest carpenters and upholsterers in Faerûn. They were brought to the castle through the portal from Talis the White's lodge.

This front chamber serves Rezmir as an office. It contains a writing desk, several smaller tables stacked with inventories and reports, and four beautiful but uncomfortable wooden chairs. Two matched onyx carvings of black dragons flank the top of the staircase. A serious collector would pay up to 3,000 gp for the pair. They are three feet tall and weigh 400 pounds apiece.

Among the papers on the desk are Rezmir's notes describing the portal beneath the castle and how to operate it, including its command word ("Draezir").

3M. Rezmir's Sitting Room

This chamber is a sitting room, comfortably furnished with upholstered chairs, padded benches, and two small carpet-draped tables. Rezmir does not entertain guests, so the chamber is never used by anyone but her.

3N. Rezmir's Sleeping Chamber

A large bed, two wardrobes, a standing mirror, and an armor stand with a spare suit of scale mail armor dominate the room. One of the wardrobes is filled with clothing. The other, whose doors are painted with a depiction of a five-headed dragon, contains Rezmir's Cult of the Dragon regalia—purple robes, cloaks, mantles, and many items of rank, but not the *Black Dragon Mask*. Because Rezmir is a half-dragon, it's unlikely that her clothing or armor will fit anyone else.

The wardrobe containing the cult regalia is trapped. The trap can be detected with a successful DC 20 Wisdom (Perception) check. Once spotted, the trap can be disarmed automatically by using Rezmir's *insignia of claws* or with a set of thieves' tools and a successful DC 20 Dexterity check. If the wardrobe is opened without disarming the trap or if the Dexterity check fails, the trap goes off. Vials of acid explode, causing 25 (7d6) acid damage to everyone in area 3N. Damage is halved with a successful DC 15 Dexterity saving throw; the character who set off the trap has disadvantage on the saving throw. All Cult of the Dragon items in the wardrobe are ruined by acid, as are most of the furnishings and other objects in the room, including the dragon statuette described below.

One of the few easily portable items of value in the room is a 2-foot-tall statuette of a black dragon, made from actual black dragon scales and claws, with ruby eyes and diamond teeth. It is perched atop a heap of treasure consisting of actual gold and gems. Its value to a collector is 4,800 gp, and it weighs only 20 pounds. Rough handling will damage it, however, and reduce its value to just 1,200 gp.

Castle Naerytar
Level 3
Blando

□ Equals 20 Feet

is empty of all but their reed mattresses and belongings in wooden trunks. A small stone hearth provides meager warmth. The door to area 3S is always kept closed but not locked.

3S. UNUSED ROOM

A portion of the roof and northwest wall has collapsed in this chamber, so it isn't used for anything. The door to area 3R is always kept closed but not locked.

3T. CULTISTS' STUDY

The six cultists who share area 3R use this chamber for studying their spellbooks and for practicing their magical craft. The chamber is empty except for three stools, three writing desks, and a basin of water.

3U. OBSERVATORY

The Stargazers converted the top level of the keep into an astrological observatory. The most interesting device they installed was a *farseer of Illusk*—a telescope-like contraption that is useful for observing and studying heavenly bodies but which can also be used in a manner similar to an *arcane eye* spell. In that mode, the *farseer* can view a location within fifty miles of it. Tuning and focusing the device this way calls for a considerable amount of skill and practice, and the device's dilapidated condition makes the process more difficult.

Both Rezmir and Borngray visit this area frequently to study the *farseer*. The elf has had limited success with it, but Rezmir has mastered its use. Over the past year, she used the *farseer* to study Voaraghamanthar in the dragon's lair. During those spying sessions, Rezmir discovered the dragon's secret twin.

To protect this area, Rezmir enlisted the service of four **gargoyles**. They perch day and night on the four corners of the keep's roof, where they can be seen from the ground and where they can see through windows into the observatory. Only Rezmir and Borngray know the gargoyles are alive. If anyone enters the observatory without being accompanied by one of the two cult officers, the gargoyles tear open the observatory's four ceiling hatches and attack. This is the only intrusion they respond to. The gargoyles don't interfere elsewhere without direct orders from Rezmir, and she won't give such an order unless it is the direst of emergencies.

A character who inspects the contents of the

3O. REZMIR'S SANCTUARY

This chamber is where Rezmir retires to venerate Tiamat privately. The room is bare. Its only decoration is a stylized depiction of a five-headed dragon rising from a volcano, painted on the back of the door (where it won't be seen unless someone closes the door while they're in this room). The artist had only a few colors to work with and was not especially talented, but the five heads are recognizable as the five chromatic dragons.

3P. KITCHEN STORAGE

This room contains more kitchen storage, similar to area 2P. Only dry goods are kept here—flour, sugar, dried fruits and vegetables—to avoid the hassles of hauling tubs or barrels of liquid up the stairs.

3R. CULTISTS' SLEEPING CHAMBER

Middle-ranking cultists have the entire top floor of the tower for their use. At night, six **dragonwings** (see appendix B) are present. Otherwise, the chamber observatory recognizes the *farseer of Illusk* with a successful DC 15 Intelligence (Arcana) check. After its true nature is ascertained, using it to view a distant location requires a successful DC 15 Intelligence (Arcana) check and a successful DC 15 Dexterity (Sleight of Hand) check. If the Intelligence check fails, the desired location can't be found. If the Dexterity check fails, the image is too distorted to convey any information. If the Dexterity check result is 5 or less, a key part of the *farseer* breaks off, rendering the item inoperable.

When characters find it, the *farseer* is focused on Waervaerendor's lair. This is a golden opportunity for characters to learn Voaraghamanthar's secret.

Characters might try to take this item when they leave. The *farseer* is bulky (approximately 40 pounds of brass, crystal, and wood) and fragile (with crystal lenses for focusing and delicate gears in the tuning mechanism). Worst of all, it has suffered almost two centuries of neglect and exposure. The least amount of rough handling will shatter its brittle workings and ruin it. A team of brass-smiths and sages, working patiently, might be able to remove the device from Castle Naerytar intact, but adventurers working in haste have no chance.

Beneath the Castle

The caverns beneath Castle Naerytar are accessible through area 1S. At the top, the steps are smooth and well made. As they descend, they are rougher, make several turns, and descend about 20 feet to area 1 of the dungeon map. This subterranean area is largely the realm of the bullywugs, who breed giant frogs in the cold lake. Pharblex spends most of his time down here, as do his bodyguards and many workers.

General Features of the Cave

Everywhere the walls drip water and the floor is slick with moisture. The temperature is a steady 50 degrees. There are no doors in the caverns.

Ceilings. Cavern ceilings are 10 feet high except where noted otherwise.

Light. Area 1 is brightly lit by lanterns. All other areas have no light.

Sound. The caverns are filled with the faint sounds of dripping water, scratching rodents, and scrabbling lizards. Sound does not carry well; the sound of a fight travels into neighboring chambers and attracts attention if the fight lasts more than three rounds.

1. Entry Cavern

The steps down from the southwest tower of Castle Naerytar spill out into this chamber. The chamber is brightly lit by one lantern hanging next to the entrance steps and another hanging near the northwest opening to area 9. The chamber is empty. Only the sound of dripping water comes from the direction of areas 3 and 9.

Steps to the northwest descend 5 feet to area 9. Steps to the southeast ascend 5 feet to a passage that descends again 5 feet to area 3. A search for muddy footprints accompanied by a successful DC 10 Wisdom (Perception) check reveals that only bullywugs use the southeastern passage, never cultists or lizardfolk.

The water flooding the center of the chamber is little more than a puddle; it reaches a depth of 1 foot near the center. The water is slightly acidic, but not enough to cause damage. The gap in the wall connecting to area 2 is only about 3 feet high above the water, so most characters must crouch to get through.

2. Gray Ooze Lair

This chamber is the lair of a **gray ooze**, though none of the bullywugs or cultists are aware of it. Occasionally it slithers out of its chamber and eats a giant frog; the rest of the time, it stays out of sight. The ooze matches the surrounding stone perfectly and has nothing but time in which to camouflage itself. Compare the ooze's Dexterity (Stealth) check to the characters' passive Wisdom (Perception) scores to determine whether one or more of them spots it.

Searching characters do see the glint of gems beneath the water at the east end of the chamber. Fishing through that area turns up a handful of fancy and semi-precious stones worth 1,800 gp (2 × 50 gp, 5 × 100 gp, 200 gp, 400 gp, 600 gp). The gems came from a less-than-devoted cultist who throws a fistful of coins and other treasure items into area 2 every time he gets the chance. His plan is to come back to the castle after the cult leaves and collect his "retirement fund." Unknown to him, the ooze living in area 2 scoops up the items when it passes through its lair. All the items except the gems dissolve in the ooze's body. The stones fascinate the creature's tiny brain, so it "spits out" the gems in the corner and collects them. The ooze won't bother those who enter, look around, and leave. It fights back if attacked, and it attacks (probably with surprise) anyone who takes gems.

3. Mud Room

The floor of this room is flooded a foot deep with sticky, reeking mud, making the whole chamber difficult terrain. Bullywugs roll in this mud, both because they enjoy it and for obscure ceremonial purposes mandated by Pharblex. Two **bullywugs** maintain the mud at just the consistency and depth the bullywugs prefer. They don't leap to the attack when characters enter, but they are hostile and quick to anger.

The steps to the west descend steeply 10 feet to area 4. A lip of stones across the top of the steps keeps most of the mud from spilling down the steps, but enough slops over to make the steps slippery. Every character who walks down these steps must make a successful DC 8 Dexterity saving throw to avoid tumbling into area 4. The fall causes 1d4 bludgeoning damage and makes a lot of noise.

4. Centipede Lair

This chamber is empty, but swarms of centipedes live in niches and alcoves lining the western wall. They are frightened away by torches, but lanterns, candles, and *light* spells don't bother them. They attack any group that isn't carrying at least one lit torch. There are two **swarms of centipedes** per party member.

EQUALS 10 FEET

BLANDO

5. EMPTY CHAMBER

The steps to the west descend 5 feet to area 6.

6. FROG LAKE

Pharblex and the bullywugs raise giant frogs in this water-filled cavern. The ceiling arches 30 feet overhead. The floor of the pool drops off suddenly from the shore, with the water varying from 10 to 15 feet deep.

When characters enter, a **giant frog** sits still on the island and watches them. Most characters can't see that far from the entrance with torches or lanterns. If the characters stick to the shore between the east and north entrances, the frog doesn't react. If someone enters the water or walks out onto the promontory, the frog croaks loudly and splashes into the water. Characters hear more croaking and at least a dozen splashes from area 7. If they are still in area 6 or area 7 after 2 rounds, they are attacked by twelve **giant frogs**. The frogs focus their attacks on small characters they can swallow.

Frogs move into and out of this area by swimming through a passage that opens below the water level in the southeast corner of the pool. Characters can deduce this fact if they watch the pool for 10 to 15 minutes and make a successful DC 12 Intelligence (Nature) check. The passage connects to water south of the bullywugs' huts outside the castle. Its total length is 300 feet. At 80 feet from the entrance in this pool, the tunnel branches;

the left branch leads to the surface and the right branch extends 50 feet to a dead-end. In the pitch blackness, a swimmer has few cues about which tunnel to follow. A DC 15 Intelligence (Investigation) check reveals which tunnel to follow.

Many bats also roost in this cavern. They can reach the outside through natural chimneys in the roof. The bats don't bother anyone normally, but if a fight breaks out, they become agitated and fill the air.

7. FROG LANDING

When they aren't swimming in the underground lake, most of the giant frogs in the cavern sit on this rocky shelf, occasionally snatching bats out of the air with their long tongues. There can be as many as twelve **giant frogs** here at a particular time, plus up to five **bullywugs**. The bullywugs don't join the fight if the giant frogs attack characters as described in the area 6 description. Instead, they dive into the water and watch the fight from the edge of the characters' light. If the giant frogs look likely to win, the bullywugs join in. If the giant frogs lose, the bullywugs swim for the underwater exit in the southeast corner of the pool (see area 6).

Bones of larger animals brought here by the bully-wugs and fed to the frogs also litter the ground. Most disturbing of all are three sets of iron shackles anchored to the stone, with human, elf, dwarf, and halfling bones.

8. TADPOLE HATCHERY

Giant frog tadpoles are raised in this small pool until they are large enough to avoid being eaten by the adult frogs in areas 6 and 7. The tadpoles currently in this area are harmless to characters.

The passage from area 6 is guarded by two **bullywugs** to keep adult frogs out. They hide from enemies in area 6 if they can. They'll fight if cornered or if a fight develops in area 6 and they see a chance for victory.

9. CRANE

The ledge dividing area 9 from area 10 is a 15-foot drop. A wooden, crank-powered crane has been set up for lowering heavy crates of treasure down to area 10. The crane effectively triples a character's Strength score in terms of how much weight can be lifted. A wooden ladder is lashed to the ledge for climbing up and down.

10. MISTY ROOM

Mist flowing out of area 2 and through area 9 accumulates here to a depth of 3 feet before spilling into area 6 and dissipating. Otherwise, the chamber is empty.

11. FROG SHRINE

Pharblex turned this area into a shrine to his distorted notions of religion. Niches in the walls are filled with carvings of frogs ranging from the size of a fist to the size of a pumpkin. Larger carvings sit on the floor. Crude renderings of frogs are scratched into the walls around the niches and colored with chalk.

Anyone with the Intelligence (Religion) skill recognizes elements in these designs taken from the worship of both Ghaunadaur (god of slimes) and Shar (goddess of shadows), but none of these elements are used in a canonical manner. Pharblex used pieces that he saw in religious icons that arrived in treasure shipments, but he has no understanding of their real meaning. With a successful DC 18 Intelligence (Religion) check, a character also sees indications that Ramenos is venerated here. Ramenos is an ancient entity now believed to be in a deep slumber. As far as the character is aware, Ramenos was a god of one of the ancient creator races—if it was ever anything more than a legend. Judging from this chamber, whoever created this place has only the shallowest knowledge about these entities.

Unless a disturbance develops elsewhere in the caverns, the most likely place to find Pharblex is here, followed by areas 12 and 7 (in that order). Wherever he goes, **Pharblex** has ten **bullywugs** protecting him.

12. PHARBLEX'S SANCTUM

Pharblex comes to this chamber to contemplate the great mysteries of the universe—or so he tells his followers. This is the only place Pharblex goes alone. His bodyguards wait in area 10 or 11 while Pharblex "communes with the great powers." The chamber contains a mud-covered chair and reading table, a box of candles, and a wooden chest.

The chest is not locked, but it is trapped. If the chest is moved or if the hasp is not opened properly, six clay pots drop from concealed niches in the ceiling. Roll a d6 to determine how many pots shatter on the floor. The pots contain fine powder coated with hallucinogenic frog poison. Every creature in the chamber that is neither a frog nor a bullywug must make a Constitution saving throw with a DC equal to 11 + the number of pots that broke. A creature that succeeds on the save is unaffected. A creature that fails the saving throw succumbs to the hallucination that all other creatures in the chamber have been transformed into nightmarish, frog-like monstrosities. While affected, the creature cannot take reactions and must roll a die at the start of each of its turns. If the die result is odd, the creature must use its action and all of its available movement to move to area 6, enter the pool, and remain underwater. If the die result is even, the hallucinating creature attacks the nearest creature to it, treating it as hostile. The effect lasts for 10 minutes.

The trap can be spotted by someone who inspects the chest or the ceiling and succeeds on a DC 12 Wisdom (Perception) check. Unbroken clay pots can be saved and used as poison grenades. A pot has a 50 percent chance to break open any time it's thrown. Bullywugs and frogs of all kinds are immune to the poison's effect.

Pharblex retires to this chamber to study two spellbooks, which he stole from area 2N. Dralmorrer Borngray and Rezmir would be furious if they learned the books were missing. One belonged to a 7th-level wizard and contains spells up to level 4, and the other was written by a 9th-level wizard and contains spells up to level 5 (you pick the spells). Being wizard spells, the magic is beyond Pharblex's ability to learn or cast; his lust for power is great enough to keep him puzzling over the text and hoping for a breakthrough.

13. TO THE GRAYPEAK MOUNTAINS

Mist from area 10 seeps into this room and keeps it filled to a depth of two to three feet. Aside from the mist, the chamber appears empty.

It is not empty, however. A permanent teleportation circle is carved into the floor, where it is obscured by the mist. Characters with a passive Wisdom (Perception) score of 10 or higher spot the circle, while dispersing the mist (using a gust of wind spell, for example) reveals the circle to all.

To travel through the gate, a command word must be spoken aloud (a whisper will do). The command word ("Draezir") can be found on a paper on Rezmir's desk in area 3L or from Dralmorrer Borngray if he faces defeat with no escape. When the command word is spoken, everyone and everything inside the gate's circumference is teleported to the corresponding gate in the hunting lodge of Talis the White (see episode 7). Castle Naerytar and the Graypeak Mountain lodge were constructed by the same reclusive wizard, and this was his means of transit between the two.

REWARDS

Award standard XP for defeated foes. If you are using the milestone experience rule, the characters reach 6th level after activating the gate.

EPISODE 7: HUNTING LODGE

Characters who follow Wyrmspeaker Rezmir or Azbara Jos with the aid of the teleportation circle in Castle Naerytar's dungeon are deposited high in the Greypeak Mountains. The change in climate is very stark; the portal and a nearby lodge are buffeted by chill winds, and the surrounding countryside is heavily forested. The portal is one of several that predate the Cult of the Dragon, and it helps the cult leaders gather over large distances.

Next to the portal is a hunting lodge used by a succession of local lords over the years. The lodge is a useful and central meeting place for high-ranking cultists, among them a Wearer of Purple known as Talis the White.

Talis feels strongly that she belongs in Severin's "inner circle," but Severin doesn't trust her and recently appointed a dwarf named Varram as his wyrmspeaker in charge of recovering the *White Dragon Mask*. The adventurers meet Talis and her servants, and they could end up fighting Talis and her crew in the lodge. They might also bargain and make a deal with Talis, striking against those who oppose her ascension. If they do the latter, she helps the party reach the nearby village of Parnast and aboard Skyreach Castle (see episode 8)— but negotiations are fairly hazardous and might easily result in combat rather than a deal.

If the players don't realize that the cult hopes to bring Tiamat to the Realms, this episode is the best time for that information to be revealed or confirmed. Although Talis won't mention any details such as masks or summonings, the cultists share a general belief that the time is right for Tiamat's arrival. The characters can find several clues that encourage this belief.

GENERAL FEATURES

The lodge is built in a comfortable but rustic style, and good tapestries and some hunting trophies festoon its rooms. The wooden floors are heavily scarred by claws. A successful DC 20 Intelligence (Nature) check reveals that these are not the marks of normal hunting hounds, but rather ambush drakes (see appendix B).

Ceilings. Most hunting lodge ceilings are 8 feet high.

Light. The lodge is not lit except by fireplaces and candles. The interior is dark when the shutters are closed.

IMPORTANT NONPLAYER CHARACTERS

The cultists who meet in the lodge come and go around planned gatherings. At the moment, things are in a lull.

TALIS

Talis believes she is the rightful bearer of the *White Dragon Mask*, and that she was deeply wronged when custody of the mask went to her hated rival, the dwarf Varram, a foolish creature whom Talis considers insultingly incompetent and worthless. She's been watching the cult's hoard grow, and she hopes to still make her move to become a major figure within the cult hierarchy—certainly she has a lot of support among cultists.

REZMIR

Because they are enemies, Rezmir does not warn Talis that attackers might be coming through the portal on her heels, but instead slips off to Skyreach Castle (see episode 8) with the intent of letting the adventurers destroy Talis. If the characters slew Rezmir, the lodge's relative lack of watchfulness is not surprising.

If Rezmir survived the earlier episode, the half-dragon meets with Captain Othelstan in Parnast to receive a full report on the status of the cult raids and to inform the captain of the possible arrival of adventurers. Tracking her successfully requires a DC 23 Wisdom (Survival) check. If the adventurers ignore the lodge in favor of following Rezmir to Parnast, skip to episode 8.

TREPSIN THE TROLL

This four-armed troll is a demon-worshiper and a fanatical hunter of big game: nothing pleases him so much as bringing blood and bones back to feed his ambush drakes, or the delightful terror of his more intelligent victims. Trepsin cares mostly about combat and mayhem, but he has found that serving the cult makes combat and mayhem more likely. He's very devoted to Talis, and he serves the Cult of the Dragon enthusiastically. His four arms just make it easier to claw, rip, and shred anything too slow to escape his reach. He terrifies the kobolds and the human servants of the lodge.

> ### CULT SIGNS AND SIGNALS
>
> The Cult of the Dragon uses several signs and countersigns among its members, the most common being holding the hand out with all five fingers extended, which they call the "Tiamat salute." In addition, the phrases "All hail Tiamat!" and "They shall rise!" are frequently used pass phrases.
>
> In addition to their signals, cultists often wear a five-colored band or even use red, blue, and green stripes as coded bits of clothing. A few banners showing cult insignia also exist, but most of those are being held in reserve for the days when the dragons rise to take over. Until then, pass phrases and the salute are the recognition signals most used among Cult of the Dragon members.

THROUGH THE GATE

The gate from Castle Naerytar closes as soon as the party steps through. The gate cannot be reopened without the proper password.

> Dark pine woods are all around on the slopes of a mountain valley; the air is cold and fresh. Two ancient stones stand to either side of you, and no more than a bowshot ahead along a path is a large house, with stone on the ground floor, timbers above. Within sight are more standing stones.
>
> Pine branches shift and sway in a gusting, fitful wind. A squirrel chitters and then falls silent.

The portal stands between stone markers (see area 1).

OUTSIDE THE LODGE

> This ancient building has a wood and plaster upper floor over a fieldstone lower floor: its shuttered windows are all closed. The roof is completely overgrown with moss. A single door stands slightly open. Smoke pours from one of three large chimneys.

The lodge stands in a distant woodland, among tall pines and in excellent hunting territory. The building can be accessed through the front door, kitchen door, the shuttered windows (DC 10 Dexterity check or a shutter bangs), or a hole in the moss-covered roof (above area 17) that's visible from the kennel and stables. Climbing up to the hole requires a successful DC 15 Strength (Athletics) check.

The drake kennel (area 2) and wyvern stables (area 3) are stone outbuildings located behind the lodge, near a well and a woodpile. Investigating the kennel rouses the loud hissing and peculiar deep growl of drakes, and is one sure way to get the entire lodge's attention.

There's also the peryton nest on the roof (see area 22), directly above area 18.

OUTDOOR PATROL

If the party lingers outside the lodge or explores the woods nearby, it finds company. Those with a passive Wisdom (Perception) score of 12 or higher are not surprised by the rush of a group of two **trolls** and three **ambush drakes** (see appendix B) that has been wandering the area. The combat alerts Talis that she has company. The trolls serve as the lodge's bouncers, and anyone who is not expected is eaten.

TROLL PURSUIT

If the party is forced to retreat from the lodge, the four-armed **troll** Trepsin (see area 2) pursues them and tries to bring at least one of them back to the lodge for questioning.

1. Portal Stones

> The mossy stones are old and weathered; lichen covers most of their surfaces, but traces of white paint remain in a few of the grooves.

The magical gate to Castle Naerytar sits between a pair of moss-covered standing stones visible from all the front rooms of the lodge. Three other portals near the lodge stand between similar stones, and the cultists have re-tuned their destinations to suit their own ends. One of them connects to the distant north (where Talis visits white dragon allies), one leads to a heavily guarded chamber in Thay, and one leads to the desert of Mulhorand, near a blue dragon lair.

These additional portals should not be a major part of the adventure, but they can introduce cultist nonplayer characters coming to "do business at the lodge" if the characters decide to dawdle at the lodge for many days. Activating any of these portal stones is unlikely without the lore available in distant libraries or in Rath Modar's chambers in Skyreach Castle (see episode 8).

TREPSIN

The grooves are Draconic letters that spell out words in Loross, the language of Netheril. They mention the "snowy lands," an "unquiet swamp of mournful croaking," and the lands of the "red sun," but provide no place names. Over time, the stones have been used to reach many sites within the Realms.

2. Hunting Kennel

> The stone outbuilding has a mossy roof and no windows. The solid oak doors at either end are 9 feet tall; the whole thing resembles a small barn.

Opening the door requires a *knock* spell or a successful DC 20 Strength check; hammering on it brings the occupants over to open it, but they might be a surprise. When the door opens, read:

> The door opens and the smell of rotting flesh wafts out. The creature just inside the door is a four-armed troll in a muddy cloak, holding the leash of a small dragon. "What you want?" it asks. "Show the sign."

The four-armed **troll**, Trepsin, is asking for the cult's recognition signal. If the characters don't know it or just don't provide it, the troll attacks.

The kennel contains six **ambush drakes**, which the cultists use to track and kill game and intruders. The drakes obey Trepsin as the leader of their pack.

Trepsin wears a mossy and filthy cape that he soaks in water from the well; this provides both good camouflage and partial protection against fire. The muddy cape allows him to ignore the first 10 points of fire damage from any attack or source.

If the characters investigate the interior of the kennels, they find a disturbing altar.

> At the back of the kennels, three boar spears have been lashed together in a rough and strong tripod. An animal carcass hangs from the tripod by a rope: probably a young boar, though the flies make it hard to tell. Beneath it is a bowl circled by runes written in blood.

The runes are written in Giant. Trepsin is a follower of the demon lord Baphomet, lord of hunters and slayers. The strange and rusted spear-altar has rotted meat on it as a sacrifice to the demon lord.

Treasure

Trepsin keeps some items for himself. These include six ermine pelts (100 gp each), three fox pelts (25 gp each), and the prize of his collection: a full winter wolf cloak (250 gp) with a mithral clasp in the shape of a paw used to secure the cloak (750 gp).

3. Stables and Well

The stables sometimes hold a wyvern or three, but they are empty at the moment. The well has a hoist, a bucket, and cold water, and it seems to have been carved magically through stone. It is otherwise unremarkable.

Lodge Ground Floor

The lower floor has heavy, mud-stained carpets and dark wooden walls. These are the common spaces for visitors and for servants. Characters can enter the lodge through the front door, the kitchen door, or a shuttered window. Opening a shutter without alerting the lodge's occupants requires a successful DC 12 Dexterity (Stealth) check.

The lodge is currently empty of most senior cultists other than Talis, who is on the upper floor (see area 16). She expects only fellow cultists as visitors. Most servants will expect that friendly visitors are here to see her.

4. Cloak Room and Guard Post

The entryway is empty most of the time.

> Just inside the front door is a chamber with pegs and benches for cloaks and boots. A set of rusty spears rests in one corner, held in the claw of a small drake statue.

The guard post to the right of this entryway is unoccupied except when large groups of rival cultists gather. Two small arrow slits make it easy to fire into the entry hall with three-quarters cover.

5. Small Hall

> This central hallway has stairs, large wooden doors, and a set of fine plate armor. Flanking the main entrance are two freestanding suits of elven plate armor, both coated in chipped green paint. Man-sized demonic statues stand near the base of the stairs.

The heavy carpet near the entryway is stained with the muddy boots of returning hunters. The two demonic statues are **gargoyles**, and they attack creatures that enter the hall with weapons drawn.

Treasure

The freestanding suits of elven armor are warded with freezing runes that can be detected with a successful DC 20 Wisdom (Perception) check. Any character that touches one of the suits or passes between them must make a DC 15 Constitution saving throw. On a failed saving throw, the character takes 1d12 cold damage and is restrained (frozen in place) for 1 minute. The character may use an action on his or her turn to make a DC 15 Strength check, ending the effect early on a success.

Each suit of plate armor is mounted on a crude wooden stand vaguely shaped like a headless elf. A freezing rune can be remove with *dispel magic* (DC 15), whereupon the armor becomes nonmagical.

6. Three Hounds Parlor

> The stout beams overhead are stained black with smoke. A comfortable table and chairs, a small wardrobe, and suit of dull black armor stand in the room. A large tapestry shows three hounds dragging down a white boar, and it shimmers with strange light.

The black armor is a **helmed horror** built to serve the cult, and disguised by an illusion to appear as ordinary armor. It detects as magical and attacks if disturbed or if commanded to do so by Talis or someone else wearing purple Cult of the Dragon robes.

The helmed horror has an *Evard's black tentacles* spell stored in it. It is programmed to cast this spell when confronted by three or more adversaries, and can do so only once. (See the helmed horror's stat block for details on its Spell Storing trait.)

The tapestry is magical and transports those who step through it into the surrounding forest, about five miles from the lodge. It often places the travelers near a deer, mountain goat, or other wild game.

The tapestry weighs about 50 pounds and works only when it is hanging on a wall, teleporting creatures to a random location out to a range of five miles; it does not work if placed on the floor like a carpet and loses its magical property if damaged in any way. It is worth 2,500 gp, or 400 gp if it loses its teleportation property.

7. Kitchen

There is a door out to the drake kennels (area 2) and well (area 3) here.

> This spacious kitchen is a hive of activity. A large stove against one wall contains a roaring fire with a bubbling stew pot and shanks of venison suspended above it. Strings of onions and herbs crisscross the ceiling like webs above cluttered tables. Preparing meals are four humans: two men and two women. All are within arm's reach of boiling water, cleavers, and knives, and their stares make it quite clear they don't like company.

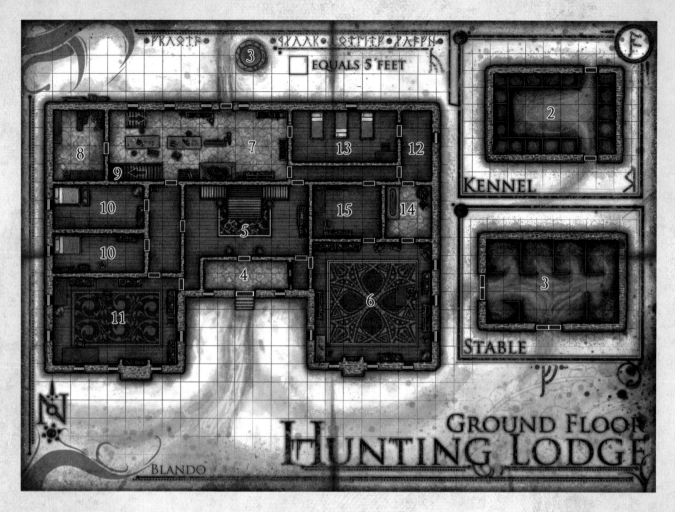

GROUND FLOOR
HUNTING LODGE

BLANDO

These four **cultists** are Talis's servants. They know how to cook, and they can put up a fight. If attacked, one cultist runs to the drake kennels (area 2) to fetch Trepsin and his drakes. Those reinforcements arrive 3 rounds later.

8. PANTRY

This pantry is well-stocked with beans, butter, smoked hams, hard biscuits, fresh apples, eggs, sacks of flour, and barrels of ale. There's enough food here to last a long winter.

A successful DC 18 Intelligence (Investigation) check reveals a hollow space under the floorboards that contains a strongbox, inside which is stored the lodge's fine dining silver: 24 place settings of butter knife, soup spoon, fork, and dessert spoon—but no knives. The silver is worth 300 gp all told, and it weighs 50 pounds.

9. BASEMENT

The cellar is damp and smells like apples and vinegar. Bags of apples and sacks of potatoes line one wall. Three prisoners are chained along another wall: a dwarf with a chopped and singed beard, and two humans—a man and a woman. The woman is wounded. Their chains are secured to iron rings, keeping them just out of reach of the food.

They are all shackled with iron chains and malnourished, and two of the captives are clearly whipped and beaten. The cultists captured them and brought them to the lodge for interrogation.

Craggnor the Dwarf. Craggnor is a member of the cult and a friend of the dwarf Varram the White, the cultist whom Talis hates above all others. She captured Craggnor hoping to learn a weakness she can exploit, but so far he has resisted various bribes, enchantments, and physical torments. She intends to try a more powerful form of mind-reading after she can pull together materials.

Miresella. This young woman from Baldur's Gate came to Parnast with a caravan, stumbled upon the cult's doings here, and was captured. She is terrified of Talis, who comes down to beat her and Craggnor from time to time. She has bruises and cuts along her neck and shoulder. Treat her as a human **scout** with just 1 hit point to start. She's grateful to escape but not eager to tangle with the cult unless healed and equipped.

Brother Caemon. This human **priest** of Amaunator has not been scourged, beaten, enchanted, or otherwise abused, which frankly seems to make him a little nervous. He says he arrived here from Hillsfar to the east, as part of a pilgrimage to a shrine on the coast, and this is why Talis singled him out for good treatment—he's unlikely to know anything useful.

Brother Caemon suspects that Talis is trying to win him over to the cult, but he also fears that Talis plans to sacrifice him as part of a summoning ritual and is trying the "catch more flies with honey" approach to win his freedom. Talis's kindness is entirely false, but it might confuse the characters as a red herring. Caemon doesn't know much, and he is a bit of a kind-hearted fool.

10. Guest Chamber

> This room is dark and cold. Furnishings include a bed covered with blankets and furs, a small desk with an unlit oil lamp atop it, a washstand, a chamberpot, and a brazier of coals. The window is shuttered.

This room is ready for guests, but unoccupied. There are no valuables beyond bedding, furs, and similar items.

11. White Stag Parlor

> This room is warm and comfortable, with a large fireplace, stuffed leather chairs, and a table set with smoked sausages and candles. A tapestry displays a magnificent white stag above a valley, with a pair of green dragons soaring overhead and deer, boars, and hedgehogs hiding among the leaves and trees below.
>
> The walls each have a trophy or two, including two fine mountain goat heads, an elk's head with a 10-point rack, a giant eagle's head and talons, a metallic bull's head, a griffon's head and foreclaws, and the head of a white-furred boar with tusks as long as daggers. The room seems otherwise deserted.

The tapestry here is worth about 400 gp, but weighs 40 pounds. The metallic bull's head is a gorgon, and the trophies are all real, though not especially valuable except as curiosities. The griffon's head does contain something unusual: a stash of two *potions of healing*.

12. Kobold Servants

> A foul odor permeates this unfurnished room, which is filled with more than twenty kobolds, half sleeping and half awake.

The twenty-four **kobold servants** are the lodge's maids, grooms, sweeps, laundry, and cooks. They work primarily at night. The servants avoid combat, but they spy on every visitor and report back to Talis if they see anything suspicious.

13. Human Servants

> This room contains three beds and a simple writing desk. The room smells clean, and the floorboards are swept spotless.

Three human servants (**commoners**) sleep here when they are not working as the lodge's waiters and greeters. They were hired by the lodge's prior owner, one Lord Marsten, a noble slain by the cult. They are confined to this chamber when not serving Talis. These resentful servants are the chief butler Gastyn, head maid Arlaenga, and former chief hunter and now chief groom Angrath Woodwise. They resent the cultists, especially Trepsin the troll.

The human servants avoid combat, but they spy on every visitor. Arlaenga is trying to ingratiate herself, and she reports back to Talis if she sees anything suspicious.

The servants are willing to tell the adventurers about the troll in the kennels (area 2) and the room where the whole cult comes to plot (area 20). They also know that the perytons can be placated with food (area 22), and that the cult keeps a valuable banner in the linens (area 15). Most of all, though, they say they've seen "a castle in the sky near Parnast."

14. Bath

This small chamber has a large bathtub in it. The lower bath doubles as a laundry for the servants to wash linens, bedding, and so forth.

15. Linens

> This room is stacked with blankets, sheets, various animal furs, tablecloths, flags, banners, and rolled-up rugs.

There's nothing of exceptional value here, but one of the banners has five stripes colored black, blue, green, red, and white, respectively. The banner is meant to be flown on a lance or spear as a signal when approaching Skyreach Castle, to show that the bearer is friendly. Any captured cultist can explain the banner's purpose.

Lodge Upper Floor

The second floor includes sleeping quarters for guests, the armory, a feast hall used for cult gatherings, and Talis's private room.

16. Talis's Hall

> What looks to be a well-appointed chamber is filled with furniture and can serve as a place to eat food or discuss important matters. Three men in the room wear scale mail and carry swords; a woman wears robes over white scale mail, and she holds a wand set with a blue gemstone. "Welcome. I consider you to be my guests. Perhaps we can do business."

This encounter is the classic scene where the villain explains herself if the players are willing to pause.

Talis the White is a dangerous foe. She stands behind her bodyguards and uses a *wand of winter* (see appendix C). Talis's bodyguards include two human **veterans** named Maelgot and Sorvic, and a **dragonclaw** (see appendix B) named Kusphia. If Talis is slain, the veterans surrender, but Kusphia fights to the death to avenge her slain mistress.

Talis expects to meet some co-conspirators at the lodge to discuss various matters of her own ascendancy in the ranks. If the characters can be turned to her advantage, she would much rather send them against her rival than fight them. At the same time, she knows she cannot be seen as disloyal to the cult's interests.

Negotiating with Talis. Talis is wary of the characters but offers them hospitality to see whether they might be useful tools. An observer will note that she is polite but not warm. She seems wary but is clearly looking for something.

- **What Talis Wants.** Talis wants to move up in the ranks by causing her rivals to fail spectacularly.
- **What Talis Offers.** She urges the characters to thwart the transport of a large treasure hoard. Cultists under Rezmir's command are using a cloud giant's flying castle to expedite the delivery. Talis offers to help the characters get aboard Skyreach Castle before it departs (see episode 8) and provides them with a banner (see area 15) and a useful pass-phrase ("Tiamat, our Mother and Strength") that will allow them to reach the castle unharmed.
- **Accepting the Deal.** If the party accepts the deal, Talis prefers to remain behind so that she can use her magic to check on them from time to time. If the characters insist that she join them, she acquiesces but might turn against them depending on how events play out in Skyreach Castle.
- **Rejecting the Deal.** Refusing Talis's generous offer triggers a fight. Talis shouts for reinforcements, which brings the gargoyles from area 5, the helmed horror from area 6, and the kobolds from area 12 running, and even yells out the window for Trepsin the troll. Pull out all the stops—and if things go badly, Talis climbs out a window and flees into the woods or through a portal (see area 1).

Talis Surrenders. Talis is not a to-the-death sort of villain; she is a survivor and willing to surrender and ask for mercy. Indeed, she uses her rivalry and her recent setbacks within the cult hierarchy to paint herself as a "disgruntled cultist" who is perhaps not eager but willing to provide information.

If the characters accept her surrender, she shares the following information as long as the character questioning her continues to make a sequence of successful DC 15 Charisma (Persuasion) rolls. Once a roll is failed, she clams up—at least until she is bribed, threatened, or offered other information in exchange.

- Talis identifies the five leaders of the cult as "wyrmspeakers," each of whom has an affinity for a particular kind of chromatic dragon. The leaders' names are Severin the Red, Galvan the Blue, Neronvain the Green, Rezmir the Black, and Varram the White.
- She explains the significance of the banner in area 15 and reveals the various cult signs and signals (see the sidebar at the start of the episode).
- If that is not sufficient, she tells them that the cult has an enormous hoard of valuables in a flying castle hidden nearby—but not for long. If pressed for details, Talis reveals that castle belongs to a cloud giant allied with the cult. The castle, she says, is hidden near the village of Parnast, which is under the cult's control.
- If all that is not enough, she tells the party, in glowing and worshipful tones, that a great white dragon inhabits the castle. She refers to the dragon as "snow-white Glazhael, the Cloudchaser, a handsome dragon of the pure northern breed." She sounds like a fanatic when discussing dragonkind.
- She doesn't know much about the Red Wizards but reveals that a Red Wizard liaison has been sent to help arrange the hoard's transport to the cult's headquarters.
- She might be willing to tell the party the cult and its allies are building an army in the Sunset Mountains far to the south, in anticipation of Tiamat's arrival.

Rewards

Regardless of the outcome of the party's interaction with Talis, the characters reach 7th level for dealing with her if you are using the milestone experience rule.

17. Armory

> A gaping hole in the roof exposes this armory to the elements. Very few weapons are stored here at present. Shelves to the north lie mostly bare, and a poorly maintained weapon rack standing against the south wall holds three rusty spears and a frayed net. Nearby is a closed cabinet.

A search of the shelves and weapon rack yields a longsword, a box of 20 crossbow bolts, a box of 10 arrows, three spears, and a net. The cabinet is unlocked and contains two heavy crossbows and two longbows.

TREASURE

One of the rusty spears is decorated with inlaid mithral (50 gp), and another, named *Dragongleam*, is enchanted with 10 charges of a *daylight* spell for use in twilight or dark forest underbrush. The command phrase is "Tiamat's eyes shine," written in Draconic runes on the spear's crossguard.

18. TALIS'S BEDCHAMBER

An enormous bed is covered in a soft burgundy bedspread, and a fire crackles in the fireplace, lending the room warmth and an atmosphere of comfort.

TREASURE

Talis keeps a locked chest in this room and she carries the only key. It can also be opened by a character using thieves' tools with a successful DC 21 Dexterity check. When opened, light spills out from the *+1 chain mail* within it. The armor's light also shines on the chest's 4,000 gp and a *scroll of scorching ray*.

The two veterans carry 20 gp each, and Kusphia carries a symbol of the cult worked in silver worth 40 gp.

19. BODYGUARDS' CHAMBER

The shutters are open, allowing light to shine in. Four unmade beds line the south wall, and other furnishings include a table with four chairs and a wine rack containing a multitude of bottles, most of them uncorked and empty.

The veterans who serve Talis have taken these well-furnished quarters for their own: they are Maelgot, Sorvic, and Wessic the Wizened. Wessic, a human **veteran** of sixty years, is resting here the first time the characters show up; the others are in area 16. Wessic sleeps in his armor and keeps his weapon stowed under his bed, within easy reach. If awakened, he fights fiercely and shouts loudly for help; this usually brings Talis and the other guards, but not the Trepsin the troll or the lodge's human and kobold servants. If reduced to half his hit points, he attempts to surrender.

TREASURE

Most of the wine bottles are empty, but the twelve full ones that remain are worth 15 gp each. In addition, one of the empty bottles contains a stolen gold necklace worth 250 gp.

20. QUEEN OF DRAGONS CHAMBER

A roaring fireplace churns out heat and light at one end of this spacious, 30-foot-high chamber, the ceiling of which is buttressed by ten wooden pillars carved as dragons. Five large tapestries hang along the walls—two on the west wall flanking a door, two on the east wall hanging side by side, and a particularly grand one dominating the south wall next to the fireplace.

TALIS THE WHITE

BRYAN SYME

BLANDO

Once a feast hall, this room is now set aside for cult gatherings and is currently unoccupied. A set of double doors in the north wall pulls open to reveal a stone balcony overlooking the stables, kennel, and well (see areas 2 and 3 for details).

Tapestries. Four of the five tapestries each show dragons hunting, killing, and feasting on lesser creatures, with blue dragons attacking a desert caravan, elves succumbing to a green dragon's gaseous breath weapon, a red dragon burning down what might be the Castle Ward of Waterdeep, and a black and white dragon circling over a cold swamp dotted with ruins. Each is worth at least 500 gp to the right buyer, but each also weighs about 75 pounds and is extremely cumbersome.

The fifth tapestry shows Tiamat, the queen of evil dragons, in all her glory, crowned in gold and silver, and worked with gemstones and gold and silver thread. Fully 35 feet wide and 20 feet tall, it shows Tiamat crushing cities and surrounded by adoring followers. The tapestry weighs about 200 pounds and is worth 2,500 gp. Simply removing the semiprecious stones provides garnets, agates, moonstones, and others worth about 800 gp.

Close examination of the tapestries and a successful DC 20 Intelligence (History) check reveals their locations in the Sword Coast region. The blue dragons are attacking a caravan crossing the desert of Anauroch, the white and black dragons are circling above the Mere

of Dead Men, the red dragon is near Waterdeep, and the green dragon is clearly rampaging among the High Forest elves, based on the mountains in the background. Tiamat herself is shown with what are clearly Waterdeep, Neverwinter, and Baldur's Gate in her claws.

Secret Door. The outline of a hidden door can be found with a successful DC 20 Wisdom (Perception) check. The door opens into the trophy room (area 21).

21. TROPHY ROOM

> Three open windows let in light and air; the room's walls are adorned with stuffed animal heads, including a large 14-point stag, a mountain goat, a bear, two winter wolves, and what can only be an ankheg's head. Two tattered banners hang from the ceiling, and two leather chairs and a handful of braziers complete the comfortable parlor.

This is very much a hunter's bragging room.

Secret Door. A secret door can be discovered between the eastern tapestries with a DC 20 Intelligence (Investigate) check. The door is cunningly hidden among the room's wooden panels, and pulls open to reveal area 20. It can also be discovered by pulling on the edge of the wood panel between the tapestries.

22. Peryton Roost

> This large nest on the roof is made of woven sticks, leaves, and feathers intermingled with the sun-bleached bones of sizable animals: deer, bear, or mountain goat, perhaps.

The nest abuts a chimney that leads down to Talis's bedchamber (area 18) and belongs to a mated pair of **perytons**. Several times during the day, the perytons leave their nest to hunt for food. There's a 50 percent chance that the nest is empty during the day; at night, both perytons are roosting here.

The perytons are allies of the cult and have a clear view of the portals in front of the lodge (area 1). They cannot see the stables or kennels (areas 2 and 3) from the nest.

Combat on the Rooftop. The nest provides reasonable traction and a good perch for the perytons, but the sloped roof is tricky to stand on. At the start of its turn or whenever it takes damage, a creature standing on the roof must succeed on a DC 10 Dexterity saving throw. On a failed saving throw, the creature falls prone on the roof; if the saving throw fails by 5 or more, the creature slips and falls off the roof, taking 2d6 bludgeoning damage and landing prone on the ground.

Treasure

The nest contains bones, old bits of armor, a punctured helmet, and other detritus. Digging around for 1 minute or more also reveals two treasures: an ancient *arrow-catching shield* and a bag of tarnished silverware worth 100 gp.

Traveling to Parnast

If you are using the milestone experience rule, the characters reach 7th level after clearing out the hunting lodge and either defeating Talis or forging a tenuous alliance with her.

Walking to Parnast. The village of Parnast and the castle is a five-mile hike from the lodge, on the far side of the mountain, through forested hills, over logs and rushing creeks, and along muddy trails. It's at least a half day's walk.

Missing the Castle. If the characters kill Talis and all her servants and guardians, there's no one to tell the characters about Skyreach Castle, and the party may well delay too long healing up or investigating the lodge. Consider leaving a paper trail in Talis's personal effects, or have a villager (most villagers are cultists) show up at the lodge with a delivery of food and supplies.

DRAGONCLAW

EPISODE 8: CASTLE IN THE CLOUDS

The cult has acquired a friendly roost in Skyreach Castle, a flying fortress built by cloud giants. This castle is docked near the village of Parnast and guarded by mists, magic, and monsters. The fortress contains much of the treasure and valuables that the cult has looted from the surrounding region—treasure that will be added to an even more monstrous hoard at the Well of Dragons, where the cult plans to summon forth Tiamat.

By the time the characters arrive in the village, Rezmir has already announced that the fortress must be made ready for departure. Characters should have time to deal with Talis and possibly other cultists before it takes to the sky.

The characters must be smart in how they tackle storming the castle—it's clearly a well-fortified place. They also can't wait too long. If the characters tarry, Skyreach Castle leaves to pick up more treasure from another lair of the cult. The exact moment when it takes flight is up to you as DM.

If Talis is with the party, she can use her rank and influence to get the characters safely to Skyreach Castle, but once inside, she cannot guarantee their safety and, in fact, turns against them at the earliest opportunity. Characters should be at or near level 8 by the end of this episode.

1. Village of Parnast

This small village is secretly under the control of the Cult of the Dragon. The cultists load and unload goods here, and some of those goods are sent to Talis's hunting lodge (see episode 7).

> The village has a few dozen houses and a small square, with buildings that include a tavern, a stable, and a shrine. In contrast to this rustic burg stands a mighty ice castle half hidden in a fog-shrouded ravine: walls stand forty feet high, huge narrow towers loom upward—one of blue ice, one crumbling—and all of it is built to a scale for giants. Wisps of fog hide much of the castle's detail, but you see two statues standing just before the enormous gate.

Cultists posing as villagers are unfriendly toward visitors, while villagers under the cult's sway remain silent and withdraw from visitors for fear of incurring the cult's wrath.

If the characters demand to speak with someone in charge, they are directed to **Captain Othelstan** (appendix B) but are also warned that he has no time or patience for dealing with outlaws.

RUMORS AND INFORMATION

Laborers, porters, craftsfolk, and cultists live and work in the village, and although they are reluctant to talk, they can be bribed, charmed, or talked around with a successful DC 18 Charisma (Persuasion) check. The following bits of information are available, one for each success, and should be doled out in the order presented below.

- The highest-ranking member of the cult to frequent Parnast is the half-dragon, Wyrmspeaker Rezmir. (If she is still alive and free, Rezmir has gone into hiding. No one in the village knows where she is, although they claim that Skyreach Castle is the most likely place to find her.)
- Rezmir's deputy is a cult veteran and dragonsoul name Captain Othelstan. He commands the cult forces in Parnast, and he monitors all visitors and merchandise passing through the village.
- The cult has controlled Parnast for more than a year, and it basically brought in a company of thugs to take over.
- Some villagers were already cult infiltrators, and others signed up when it became clear that the cultists are rich and have a private army.
- The cultists keep trained wyverns in the village stables. The cultists use them to reach the castle while it is airborne. (No one in the village, including Captain Othelstan, knows where the castle goes after it leaves Parnast.)
- Characters can also learn one of two pass-phrases for safely entering for the castle from Gundalin or anyone who becomes a friendly helper to

them: "Tiamat, Our Mother and Strength" or "Hail Blagothkus."

2. THE GOLDEN TANKARD

A yellow tankard hangs over the door of this rustic tavern. Inside, though, the place is short on cheer. All conversation stops and all eyes turn in your direction. A tall, heavyset man with enormous muttonchop sideburns steps forward and asks, "What can I get you travelers?"

A visitor can buy a mug of beer for 3 cp or a mug of strong mead for 1 sp. There's sausage on the menu as well as stewed cabbage and heavy black bread (4 cp for a plate full), but no one visits for the fine dining. It's just enough to keep a visitor going another day, and no more than that.

If the characters sit and order ale, well and good.

CAPTAIN OTHELSTAN

BRYAN
SYME

coming to hunt. All the servants are making things ready for their arrival." (This is pure nonsense, of course—he has no rooms other than his own.) If the characters just wait a moment, Raggnar says he will offer them his own chambers, for a steep fee of 10 gp. "I'll clear out a few things and it is all yours." This is also a stalling tactic, though he'll certainly take the money.

Because the cultists are about to ship a castle full of treasure from the village, they desperately don't want the characters to find anything suspicious, such as wagons loaded with chests (there's no room to hide a caravan in a village this small) or their wyvern mounts in the stables (see area 3). If Raggnar can keep the characters eating and drinking and gossiping, then Skyreach Castle can slip away into the sky.

Treasure

The Golden Tankard takes its name from a magic item that Raggnar found years ago: a golden stein decorated with dancing dwarves and grain patterns. This is a *tankard of plenty.* Speaking the command word ("Illefarn") while grasping the handle fills the tankard with three pints of rich dwarven ale. This power can be used up to three times per day.

3. The Stable

> The two big doors leading into the stable are sealed, and the place looks shuttered.

If the characters ask around, the villagers claim that the stable was put out of business some time ago. Anyone listening carefully hears a bellowing noise, though (no check required). The cult keeps two **wyverns** in the stable; sometimes, they unleash a wyvern-sized roar.

Cracked sheep bones and a few ox skulls cover the stable floor. Other than riding harnesses for the wyverns, there is no treasure here.

> "I will send the pot boy out to you in a moment with the finest available in my humble tavern." He goes toward the kitchen, bellowing for a cask.

The owner is Raggnar Redtooth, who seems friendly enough but secretly takes bribes from the Cult of the Dragon. Strangers are never really welcome in his tavern, but they get service while he informs Captain Othelstan by sending a messenger. Raggnar has a violent past and is treated as an unarmored **veteran** (AC 10). He keeps his weapons behind the bar.

Prying information from Raggnar and his clientele is difficult. The villagers want to keep the characters occupied, and they ask for them to tell tales of their journey, they inquire about the characters' families and where they are from, and they query how the party got here.

If asked about a place to sleep, Raggnar makes it clear that he isn't an innkeeper: there are no beds or rooms, and even the stable is full. If anyone asks why, he gives his usual excuse: "Lord Marsten and his entourage are

> ### Wyvern Riding and Castle Catching
>
> The wyverns in the stable (area 3) are trained to carry up to two Medium or six Small riders at a time. The difficult part is getting their harnesses attached so that riders don't fall off, and giving the proper commands once airborne.
>
> Any character can put the harness on a wyvern with a successful DC 10 Wisdom (Animal Handling) check. If the check fails by 5 or more, the wyvern strenuously objects and attacks the character once with its tail stinger as a reaction. The wyverns aren't choosy about who rides them, but convincing a wyvern to fly or move in a specific direction requires an action to make a DC 15 Wisdom (Animal Handling) check; if the check fails, the wyvern ignores the rider's commands until the rider's next turn. After a rider succeeds on two such checks, the wyvern goes where the rider wants for the next hour, or until it takes damage or the rider dismounts.
>
> The castle is easily spotted, day or night, out to a range of five miles. The wyverns are faster than the castle in flight, and they can catch up to it.

DEVELOPMENTS

The characters can try to equip the wyverns with harnesses and ride them as aerial mounts; see the "Wyvern Riding and Castle Catching" sidebar for details. If they steal one or both wyverns from under the Cult of the Dragon's nose, divide 4,000 XP evenly among the characters—more than what they would receive for slaying the wyverns.

4. SHRINE OF AXES

> This wooden building is a shrine for woodcutters, and it combines several gods under one roof.

A statue of Angharradh, an obscure elven deity representing spring, stands among statues of gods representing the other seasons, namely Auril (winter), Chauntea (summer), and Mielikki (autumn). Angharradh's statue has been defaced by having her face and hands chopped away. A dead squirrel has been left at Auril's feet.

The statue of Mielikki is not only freshly painted but also has a set of small cups, bits of bread, and other small sacrifices at its feet.

5. VILLAGE WELL AND SQUARE

> A well stands at the center of the village square. Four buildings surround it: an empty shrine, a wheelwright's shop, a tavern, and a stable.

Timber merchants, woodsfolk, and others haggle over the finer lumber here, and wagons carry supplies. See areas 2, 3, and 4 for more information about the tavern, the stable, and the shrine.

The well is 40 feet deep, cold, and pure. Five human **guards** loyal to the Cult of the Dragon keep an eye out here at all times, making sure that villagers do as they are told. If the guards are confronted, one runs to fetch Captain Othelstan as the villagers flee. Only the wheelwright Gundalin sticks around to watch, and even he does so from behind a heavy wooden oxcart.

SKYREACH CASTLE

Eons ago, cloud giants built this flying fortress to take their ancient battle against dragonkind into the skies. The spirit of a giant enables it to fly—this ancient bond dates back to the days when giants and dragons fought great wars. The binding kept dragons from taking these castles for their own, and the bond still holds centuries later.

The cult has struck a bargain with the castle's owner, a cloud giant named Blagothkus who harbors no particular hatred of dragonkind (or anything else, for that matter). The spirit of his deceased wife, Esclarotta, controls the castle's propulsion and buoyancy. The cult cannot afford to alienate Blagothkus, because the castle's spirit will not obey them.

Skyreach Castle is carved from ice so thick as to be opaque. The ice is as strong and impenetrable as granite, thanks to ancient cloud giant wizardry. Towers and walls surround an iceberg core that's been hollowed out to serve as the lair of a powerful white dragon allied with the cult. The whole thing can be hidden under a veil of fog and cloud, or set to move slowly with the wind. See area 19 for details.

GENERAL FEATURES

The castle is carved from opaque ice magically reinforced to be as hard as stone. While on the ground, the castle rests in a wide ravine on the outskirts of Parnast. Everything in the ravine is heavily obscured by fog, so the characters can approach the castle without being seen by its inhabitants. Until the castle takes flight, cultists and guards from the village deliver wagons laden with supplies and treasure to the castle's main gate (see area 6 for details).

Ceilings. All castle ceilings are 30 feet tall to accommodate the cloud giants who built it.

Doors. All doors in the castle are made of 1-foot-thick ice as hard and tough as stone, but only half the weight. They are fitted with iron hinges and handles, and sized for giants. A normal door is 20 feet tall, 8 feet wide, and has its handles situated 10 feet above floor level.

SKYREACH CASTLE

UPPER COURTYARD
16

OGRE BARRACKS
20

23

22

21

19

17

18

TO LOWER COURTYARD

SERVANTS BARRACKS

24

CHAMBERS

23   23   23

CAVE TUNNEL

☐ EQUALS 5 FEET

TUNNEL DIPS THEN UP 10'

PORCH

DOWN 30'

30 FT DOWN

DIPS DOWN 30'

25
MAIN VAULT

CEILING HOLE

DOWN 30'

UP 30'

TO LOWER COURTYARD

DOWN 40'

UP STAIRS 50'

DOWN 50'

ICE TUNNELS

SIDE VIEW

UPPER COURTYARD

LOWER COURTYARD

UPPER COURTYARD

LOWER COURTYARD

14

12

8

STABLES

10   11   13

6B

7
LOWER COURTYARD

TO UPPER COURTYARD

6A   GATE

6B

CULTIST BARRACKS

9

15

LOWER COURTYARD

BLANDO

IMPORTANT NONPLAYER CHARACTERS

Skyreach Castle is home to the cloud giant Blagothkus, a pair of stone giants named Wigluf and Hulde (allies of the cloud giant), Wyrmspeaker Rezmir of the Cult of the Dragon, two Red Wizards of Thay (Rath Modar and Azbara Jos), a vampire named Sandesyl Morgia, and an adult white dragon named Glazhael the Cloudchaser.

These adversaries do not entirely trust one another and are unlikely to present a unified front against the characters. Instead, the giants fight to defend their home, and the cultists and dragon fight to defend their treasure. If the characters play their hand wisely, this lack of trust will be the villains' undoing. The NPCs have dozens of servants, cultists, and guards at their disposal. If more than one or two of these turn up dead, the cultists search the castle for the killers.

NEGOTIATING WITH THE CLOUD GIANT

Blagothkus the cloud giant is not a particularly enthusiastic supporter of the Cult of the Dragon, but he sees it as a way to stir his fellow giants out of their complacency and into action.

Blagothkus thinks giants have grown soft, and thrashing some dragons would be good for giantkind. So, he plays along with the cult, but on the side he is gathering support among giants, urging them to assume their rightful place as lords of the world. He believes that the rise of Tiamat and the threat of a dragon empire will spur the giants to unite.

Blagothkus has no conflict with "small folk." He'll happily let the party know that yes, his castle is transporting a vast amount of treasure to the Well of Dragons, where the cult is gathering its forces and amassing a hoard in anticipation of the Tiamat's arrival (from where he doesn't know). If the characters want to help him fight cultists, he'll happily take them somewhere more interesting up north, where he's massing his own small army to fight the dragons after they have been lured out into the open. This army is further detailed in *The Rise of Tiamat*.

6. MAIN GATE

> A lowered drawbridge spans a foggy moat. Beyond the drawbridge is an open portcullis, and beyond the portcullis is a covered gateway leading to an open courtyard. Large figures loom in the gateway, but you can't quite make them out.

Prior to the castle taking flight and leaving Parnast, the cult moves a few wagons laden with treasure chests and supplies into the lower courtyard and unloads them every hour or two during daylight. Adventurers within earshot of the gate who listen closely can also hear the password spoken as each cart passes by.

The supply carts provide a way for the party to enter the castle undetected. Cultists haul the supplies to the kitchen (area 15) and carry the treasure chests down to the dragon's main hoard chamber (area 25).

WALLS AND AERIAL DEFENSES

The castle walls are carved from solid ice and possess the resiliency and texture of stone. The walls provide a great defense against attacks from the ground. While the castle is airborne, the walls also keep those within from falling to their deaths, and they block the wind.

By Day. Three **ogres** stand guard atop each gate tower (see area 6B). They can shout for reinforcements, which come from areas 9, 10, and 15. Rezmir and her guard drakes (see area 11) arrive three rounds later. The lower courtyard is clear of fog during daylight hours.

At Night. In addition to the ogres standing watch (see above), the vampire Sandesyl Morgia patrols the lower courtyard, which is heavily obscured by thick fog at night, and the upper courtyard, which is lightly obscured at night. As long as the vampire is on patrol, cultists and kobolds steer clear of the courtyards.

6A. GATEWAY AND GOLEMS

> A heavy oak-and-iron portcullis is drawn up just behind the drawbridge. Two life-sized statues of 18-foot-tall cloud giants—one male and one female—stand behind the portcullis, facing each other within the covered gateway.

The winches that raise and lower the drawbridge and portcullis are located in the nearby gate towers; see area 6B for details.

The two statues flanking the portcullis inside the gateway are **stone golems**. Anyone who passes through the gateway without speaking the correct pass-phrase ("Tiamat, Our Mother and Strength" or "Hail Blagothkus") activates one of the golems. If another creature attempts to pass through without speaking the pass-phrase, the second golem animates and attacks. Only a cloud giant can command the golems to return to their posts once activated.

6B. GATE TOWERS

> These two gate towers are not the same height. The one to the left of the drawbridge is 120 feet tall, while the one to the right of the drawbridge is 80 feet tall.

Three **ogres** stand atop each tower. Although the ogres are equipped with javelins, they can also fire their javelins from a large ballista on the roof each tower.

TOWER ROOFTOPS

It takes one action to load and fire a ballista, and a ballista can be fired only once in a given round. An ogre firing a javelin from a ballista makes the following attack instead of its regular javelin attack.

Javelin. *Ranged Weapon Attack:* +7 to hit, range 120 ft./480 ft., one target. *Hit:* 14 (3d8) piercing damage.

Each ballista has AC 10, hp 50, and immunity to poison and psychic damage.

TOWER INTERIORS

A large trapdoor in the roof of each tower can be pulled open to reveal a staircase of ice that hugs the tower interior and spirals all the way down to the tower's ground floor, where there's a single unlocked, giant-sized door leading to the lower courtyard (area 7) or the cultist barracks (area 9).

The winch that raises and lowers the drawbridge is located on the ground floor of the northern tower, while the winch for the portcullis is located in the ground floor of the other. Each winch is manned by one **ogre**, and each ogre has strict orders to guard its winch and not leave its tower even if the general alarm sounds. Turning the crank on a winch is an action and requires a successful DC 15 Strength check, and each action spent turning a crank either half-raises or half-lowers the drawbridge or portcullis. (Two actions are required to fully raise or lower either barrier.)

7. LOWER COURTYARD

The upper courtyard (area 16) partially overhangs the lower courtyard, held aloft by gigantic arches of ice. At night, the lower courtyard is heavily obscured by fog to a height of 40 feet—the same height as the walls that enclose it.

> Walls of solid ice enclose this courtyard. Another courtyard partially overhangs this one. It is held aloft by sweeping arches of ice that soar to a height of over 100 feet. Doors of sculpted ice fitted with iron hinges lead to various outbuildings and main keep on the far side of the courtyard from the gate towers.

Add the following if one or more characters succeed on a DC 22 Wisdom (Perception) check:

> Hidden in the shadows of the overhanging courtyard, across from the main gate, is an opening in one wall that leads to a spiral staircase made of sculpted ice.

Combat here alerts the ogres in area 6, the cultists in area 9, the stone giants in area 10, and the kobolds in area 15. One of the cultists runs to area 11 and alerts Rezmir, who arrives with her guard drakes three rounds later.

SPIRAL STAIRCASE

A spiral staircase of sculpted ice connects the upper and lower courtyards, as well as the tunnels leading to the main vault where the dragon lairs (area 25). The staircase's spiraling steps are coated with crunchy frost and cannot be climbed quietly, nor are they slippery.

8. STABLES

The double doors to the stables are 20 feet tall and wide, making it easy for the wyverns (see below) to get in and out.

> The place stinks of some kind of droppings and rotted flesh. Cracked bones cover the floor. Two wyverns stride into view with their fangs bared and tails lashing.

This outbuilding currently holds two **wyverns** trained as aerial mounts. However, they are hungry and attack anyone they don't recognize.

TREASURE

Four fine wyvern bridles are kept here, embellished with jade and with mithral bits (worth 500 gp each).

9. CULTIST BARRACKS

The barracks smell of unwashed bedclothes, and the chamber contains fourteen fur-covered beds, as well as several chests of clothing, a table and chairs, and other simple furnishings.

At any given time, ten **dragonwings** are resting here. Half of them are sound asleep, while the other half are awake but doing nothing overly strenuous. They do not roam the castle unless an alarm has sounded, they hear combat in the courtyard, or the ogres at the gate yell for reinforcements.

10. STONE GIANTS' CHAMBER

Two 20-foot-tall, 8-foot-wide archways connect this chamber to the lower courtyard. Any loud disturbance in the courtyard alerts the stone giants that dwell here.

> In the middle of this frost-glazed room stands a nine-foot-tall table of carved stone surrounded by three giant-sized chairs, also carved from stone. A fat iron cauldron etched with runes rests upon the table. On the floor in the far corner sits a large iron chest.

If an alarm has not been raised and the stone giants are present, add:

> A male stone giant gazes into the cauldron while a female stone giant sits nearby.

If the castle alarms have not sounded, the characters gain a surprise round.

The two **stone giants**, Wiglof and Hulda, are guests of the cloud giant. They are worried that Blagothkus's attempts to incite the giants into action against the dragons could lead to devastating consequences, but they are supportive nonetheless. They have agreed to help Blagothkus repair damage to the castle and gladly aid in its defense.

Presently, Wiglof is using a magic cauldron (see "Treasure") to perform an augury ritual and hopes to ascertain the most likely outcome of Blagothkus's alliance with the Cult of the Dragon, to either confirm or assuage the cloud giant's fears that the cult is planning to betray him. Any attack launched against Wiglof disrupts his ritual and angers him greatly. Hulda is Wiglof's companion and bodyguard, and any hostility directed at her or Wiglof is met with brutal force.

The stone giants know that the flying castle is controlled from a steering tower (area 19) accessible from the upper courtyard, and that only giants can gain entry to the tower.

TREASURE

The stone giants collect small-but-perfect gemstones, primarily amethysts but also diamonds, opals, rubies, and topaz. Their collection is secured by a magical globe of force inside an iron chest, which is six feet long, four feet tall and wide, and weighs 500 pounds. Lifting the heavy iron lid requires an action and a DC 12 Strength check, and destroying the globe of force requires an *antimagic shell* or a successful casting of *dispel magic* (DC 16). The 32 gems are worth 500 gp each, or a total of 16,000 gp. The iron chest also contains the stone giants' masonry tools, but they are neither valuable nor usable by smaller creatures.

The iron cauldron weighs 50 pounds. When filled with water or some other liquid, the cauldron substitutes for the normal material components needed to cast the *augury* spell. The cauldron is worth 25 gp.

DEVELOPMENTS

The stone giants are reluctant to share any information, but if defeated and either threatened or bribed, they might cooperate.

11. REZMIR'S CHAMBER

The door is always locked and Rezmir holds the key. A *knock* spell is the easiest way to get in, but a character can also unlock the door with a DC 25 Dexterity check made using thieves' tools. Alternatively, knocking and spinning a good yarn might work; cultists and servants come and go at all hours.

> A large rug covers the icy floor just inside the door of this 10-foot-high room, which is lit by a brazier of hot coals. A large bed rests in one corner, a desk in another. Resting atop the desk is a handsome, iron-banded chest secured with a sturdy padlock.

Unless she is lured elsewhere by a general alarm, **Rezmir** (see appendix B) is here along with two loyal **guard drakes** (appendix B).

The large rug inside of the door is actually a **rug of smothering**. The rug patiently waits for a creature to walk onto it before attacking. If they are present, Rezmir and her drakes wait for the rug to attack an enemy coming through the door before springing into action.

If Rezmir is killed, the contents of the iron chest on her desk teleport away, leaving the chest empty.

TREASURE

Rezmir carries keys to this room, the lock on the chest, and to the storeroom (area 13). In addition, the chest here is locked and magically attuned to Rezmir so that if she dies, its contents are teleported to the Well of Dragons and out of her slayers' hands.

The chest's padlock can be picked using thieves' tools with a successful DC 20 Dexterity check. However, the lock is rigged with a poison needle trap that triggers if the check fails by 5 or more. The needle can be found with a successful DC 20 Intelligence (Investigation) check and can be disarmed with a successful DC 15 Dexterity check. A creature triggering the needle trap or failing the Dexterity check by 5 or more is injected with wyvern poison and must make a DC 13 Constitution saving throw, taking 24 (7d6) poison damage on a failed save, or half as much damage on a successful one.

REZMIR

BRYAN SYME

The chest contains the *Black Dragon Mask* (see appendix C) as well as Rezmir's private collection of gems, jewelry, and coins. The gems and jewelry includes a set of matched peridot stones on a gold chain (400 gp), a silver torc with dragon's heads (200 gp), six moonstones of 50 gp each, and a set of 20 loose pearls, worth a total of 3,000 gp. There's also 600 sp, 200 gp, and 50 pp.

DEVELOPMENTS

If the characters capture Rezmir, she refuses to cooperate in any way. She prefers death over surrender, particularly if her death might keep the *Black Dragon Mask* out of her enemies' clutches (see above). Rezmir is a true believer, and the best that the characters can hope for is that their prisoner eventually stops berating and insulting them. "Your cause is hopeless. My friends will devour you, and your pitiful little attempts to deny the majesty of Tiamat will amount to nothing."

12. RED WIZARDS' ROOM

The door to this chamber is unlocked.

> Hundreds of horse skulls are nailed to the ceiling and cover it entirely. Thick carpets cover the icy floor, and desks, chairs, and lecterns are everywhere, some covered with books and scrolls, others with potion vials, bits of meat and fur, and other things. Four hulking gargoyles stand frozen in the room.

Rath Modar (see appendix B), a Red Wizard of Thay allied with the Cult of the Dragon, resides here. Unless he was killed or captured previously, **Azbara Jos** (see appendix B) is also present. If both Red Wizards are present, they are in the midst of a scholarly argument when the characters arrive, but they clam up as soon as others appear. If Rath Modar is alone, he is standing at a lectern, reading a book (see "Treasure").

If Azbara is absent, Rath Modar might mistake the characters for cultists. If the characters play along and attempt to gather information from the Red Wizard, roleplay it out. Rath is no fool, and he is an expert at seeing through illusions and deceptions. He also has a healthy suspicion of strangers, especially if the characters are wounded or inappropriately equipped.

Rath Modar is here to help watch over the vast treasure being transported to the Well of Dragons and also to plan for the summoning of Tiamat; the necessary incantations are complex and require hundreds of skilled spellcasters. He knows that the cult's ultimate goal is to free Tiamat and raise her temple from the Nine Hells, and Rath's ultimate goal is to use Tiamat and her dragons to overthrow Szass Tam.

The horse skulls on the ceiling are ghastly ornaments and nothing more.

Three of the gargoyles are statues; the fourth is a living **gargoyle** that serves Rath Modar.

Vanishing Wall of Ice. Between two windows is a 35-foot-long, 20-foot-high section of icy wall that vanishes for 1 minute when touched. Beyond the wall is an outdoor landing platform.

If he is outmatched, Rath Modar turns invisible, casts *fly* on himself, touches the disappearing wall, and leaps off the landing platform, leaving Azbara Jos to fend for himself. If the gargoyle is still alive, it tries to cover Rath's escape. His *fly* spell and disappearing trick mean that an escape is very likely.

DEVELOPMENTS

If the characters speak to Rath Modar or his associate, Azbara Jos, they find that the Red Wizard reputation for arrogance is true: the pair are haughty and proud of their skill, and they have little patience for "ruffians, thugs, and mercenaries seeking to stop the inevitable." Rath Modar and his associate figure prominently in *The Rise of Tiamat*. Defeating or killing them is a serious blow to the cult's ability to summon Tiamat.

TREASURE

Rath Modar has a scroll of *dimension door*, a scroll of *feather fall*, and a scroll of *fireball*, and he carries a *staff of fire*.

A thorough search of the room yields several letters to Rath Modar from Severin, the supreme leader of the Cult of the Dragon. Severin's letters reveal the depths of the connections between the Red Wizards (at least those friendly to Rath Modar) and the cult. The characters also find other letters from Thay revealing that clearly some Red Wizards are not nearly as keen on the cult's plans. If the characters deliver these letters to Leosin Erlanthar, Ontharr Frume, or one of their other contacts in organizations opposed to the Red Wizards and the Cult of the Dragon, award the party 1,000 XP.

Resting on a lectern is a book titled *Beyond the Iron Gates*. Written entirely in Infernal, it describes various forms of devil summoning, but the final chapter describes the use of massive summonings and the sacrifice of hundreds of souls to bring Tiamat bodily out of the Nine Hells and into the world. The details of the ritual make it clear that this is something that requires enormous preparation and expense—but the actual magical formulae and chants are not given in this volume. Neither the book nor the other papers here, however, provide a timetable for when the cult or the Red Wizards plan to attempt the summoning, nor do they mention the significance of the treasure that the cult has amassed. (Rath Modar and Azbara Jos can both attest that the treasure is to appease Tiamat upon her arrival.)

13. STOREROOM

The door is secured and locked. Any character with thieves' tools can attempt a DC 17 Dexterity check to unlock it. Rezmir and Blagothkus carry keys.

> Huge sides of beef, entire ham hocks, and enormous barrels fill this room, as do hundreds of crates. The place smells of burlap, wood, and salt.

This storeroom contains a huge amount of food, though all of it is of average quality. Other than its natural refrigeration, this room is not remarkable.

14. GUEST CHAMBER

This room is comfortably furnished for inhabitants of human size.

Vanishing Wall of Ice. A large section of the icy wall opposite the door vanishes for 1 minute when touched, exposing this room to the elements. Beyond the wall is an outdoor landing platform.

15. KITCHEN

> The scene is pure chaos: dozens of kobolds chopping, mixing, carrying sacks of ingredients, and stirring great cauldrons. It could be an alchemical lab or a kitchen—with kobolds cooking, it's a little hard to be sure.

Twenty **kobolds** are here, preparing food for the castle's other inhabitants. The kitchen is filled with huge sides of beef, entire sheep, chests full of dried fish and vast amounts of bacon, onions, beans, and so forth.

Roosting on a ledge above the fray is a **griffon**. The creature is Blagothkus's pet, and it makes sure the kobolds behave themselves. Whenever a fight breaks out, one shriek from above snaps the kobolds back in line. The griffon also protects the kobolds if they come under attack.

TREASURE

A thorough search of the kitchen reveals small chests of black pepper, cinnamon, and nutmeg. Each of these weighs 2 pounds, but their contents are worth 130 gp total.

16. UPPER COURTYARD

The upper courtyard is the primary landing site for dragons, wyverns, and flying spellcasters when the castle is airborne. During the day, 2d6 **ogres** practice their javelin hurling here. At night, the courtyard is lightly obscured by fog (to a height of 30 feet) and patrolled by the vampire, Sandesyl Morgia (see area 18).

> Tall, slender towers and walls of ice enclose a windswept courtyard.

Characters landing here need to be prepared to either show a banner or token of the cult immediately; otherwise, the ogres or vampire on watch will sound the alarm and attack them. The ogres in area 20 investigate any loud disturbance in the courtyard.

DEVELOPMENTS

If the characters arrive in disguise or fast-talk their way through the courtyard, they are taken to meet Blagothkus the cloud giant (if caught by the ogres), or Rezmir (if caught by the vampire).

17. HIGH BLUE TOWER

> This tower of pale blue ice is the color of sky on a winter day. Its few windows shimmer like mirrored glass or crystal.

The door to this tower is fitted with an iron lock, and Blagothkus carries the only key. The lock can be picked with thieves' tools and a successful DC 15 Dexterity check. Two ogres armed with javelins, rocks, and a ballista stand watch atop this tower. They have long coils of rope they use to climb up and down the tower's exterior.

The tower interior is a hollow cylinder 90 feet high, without stairs or ladders to reach the top. Any creature inside the tower that speaks the command word "Esclarotta" is instantly teleported to area 21.

DEVELOPMENTS

If the two ogres standing watch atop this tower begin firing the ballista or dropping some boulders, they get the attention of the ogre guards, cultists, and others in the main castle grounds and courtyard fairly quickly. The alarm is raised as soon as any ogre yells.

18. CRUMBLING TOWER

This tower is almost 100 feet high, but it is in shoddy repair. There are two entrances: a door at the base of the tower that cannot be opened (see below), and a working door connected to a crumbling ice balcony 75 feet above the tower's base.

> This ancient tower seems to be crumbling. The windows have been sealed shut with ice, and cracks have formed in the walls and rooftop. A balcony of sculpted ice hugs one side of the tower, 75 feet above the tower base.

This is the tower of the **vampire** Sandesyl Morgia, a moon elf who joined the Cult of the Dragon long before she became undead. She is a member of the old guard and was around long before Severin took over. Given the chance, she talks about serving under Sammaster and killing dragons to raise them as dracoliches, which she still considers "the true path." She hates the new cult leadership, but she is forced by circumstance to work with them.

Sandesyl is active by night only and prowls both the upper and lower courtyards in the night hours, keeping a keen eye out for lone ogre guards or others who might provide a meal. When confronted by more enemies than she can handle, she summons two **vampire spawn** (moon elf consorts) as reinforcements. These vampire spawn lurk on the upper floor of the tower .

The tower is in dire need of repair. The cracked and crumbled ice provides abundant handholds, allowing the tower's walls to be climbed with a successful DC 10 Strength (Athletics) check.

The tower once had four levels with 20-foot-high ceilings; however, all but the highest level have had their floors and ceilings shattered, and the staircase that once curled up the inside of the tower, connecting its various levels, has also been destroyed. The ground floor is now packed with icy debris to a depth of 20 feet, and this debris prevents the ground-floor door from being opened.

Balcony. The best way into the tower is via the balcony. However, it has been weakened and breaks away if more than 150 pounds of weight is placed on it. The door leading from the balcony is unlocked and opens into the upper level that serves as Sandesyl's crypt. There are no windows on this level.

Sandesyl's Crypt. Sandesyl's coffin rests in the middle of the tower's upper level, guarded day and night by her two consorts. The coffin contains grave dirt, but no treasure. A ice staircase hugs one wall, descending a few feet before ending suddenly, 50 feet above the icy detritus filling the lowest level of the tower.

19. STEERING TOWER

Blagothkus has secured the door to this tower with an *arcane lock*. It can be opened normally by a giant or by a *knock* spell. For everyone else, breaking it down is largely impossible, because a DC 70 Strength check is required.

SANDESYL MORGIA

BRYAN SYME

> A staircase of ice leads from the tower's ground floor to a higher chamber, the walls and ceiling of which gleam and glitter: Jewels are everywhere in the room. You see glowing moonstones, thumb-sized emeralds, shining silvery mithral wands, and strange spheres covered in turquoise and gold, as well as dozens of copper levers and golden spheres embedded in the walls. After a moment, the walls themselves seem to disappear, providing a perfect aerial view in all directions, as if there were no castle and no cloudstuff around. More than a dozen glowing white runes wink into existence, drifting about the room like snowflakes.

This is the castle's steering chamber. When no one is present, the castle is under the control of the spirit of Esclarotta, who is bound to the fortress by powerful magic that cannot be dispelled. Touching one of the glowing runes issues a specific command to Esclarotta's spirit. A character who understands Dwarvish or Giant can interpret the command runes.

COMMAND RUNES

There are eighteen command runes.

Alarm. A noise akin to a howling wind alerts all non-deafened creatures in the castle.

All-Clear. A noise akin to a loud whisper signals an end to danger.

Anchor. The castle holds position on the ground or in the air. The castle remains stationary despite winds, storms, and so on.

Cast Off. The castle is no longer anchored.

Drift. The castle drifts on the wind, effectively under no one's control.

Home. The castle returns to its place of origin, in the Spine of the World (a cold mountain range to the north).

North, South, East, and West. The castle moves in the specified cardinal direction. Touching two runes simultaneously can move the castle in other directions; for example, touching the north and east runes at the same time moves the castle northeast.

Rise. The castle ascends at a rate of 10 feet per round.

Sink. The castle descends at a rate of 10 feet per round. If it comes into contact with the ground, it lands.

Spin. The castle rotates gently clockwise, completing one full rotation in 1 minute.

Widdershins. The castle rotates gently counterclockwise, completing one full rotation in one minute.

Veil. Foggy cloudstuff materializes around the castle. After one minute, all creatures and objects in outdoor areas within 100 feet of the castle are heavily obscured, and all creatures and objects in indoor areas are lightly obscured.

Unveil. Foggy cloudstuff engulfing the castle dissipates. Lightly obscured areas become clear in 1 round, and heavily obscured areas become lightly obscured for 1 minute, then become clear.

Storm. The clouds around the castle darken and churn, becoming rumbling thunderclouds over a period of 1 minute. Until then, the calm rune cannot be activated. Once the thunderclouds have fully formed, the creature that activated the storm rune can use its action while standing in the steering chamber to target one creature it can see with a lightning bolt. The bolt has a range of 1,000 feet and can target one creature or unattended object. A creature targeted by the bolt must succeed on a DC 14 Dexterity saving throw or take 22 (4d10) lightning damage. An unattended object targeted by the bolt simply takes the damage (no saving throw).

Calm. The thunderclouds around the castle abate over a period of 1 minute. During this time, the storm rune cannot be reactivated.

Esclarotta

Although anyone can trigger command runes, the spirit of the cloud giant Esclarotta actually controls the castle and can "lock out" individuals who misuse the command runes, effectively rendering them unable to trigger the runes.

Any character succeeding on a DC 15 Intelligence (Arcana) check senses an intelligence at work, and one can attempt to communicate with Esclarotta's spirit simply by calling out to it while inside the tower. She is a kind soul, disturbed by the cultists, dragon, wyverns, and kobolds infesting her beautiful castle, and she longs for information about what her husband is up to. Requests made to her succeed with a DC 14 Charisma (Persuasion). The person has advantage on the check if he or she speaks Giant. If anyone tries to wreck the steering chamber, Esclarotta triggers the alarm rune. **Blagothkus** (see appendix B) arrives 3 rounds later with two **ogres** (his stewards) in tow.

If Blagothkus dies aboard the castle, his spirit replaces Esclarotta's, and he crashes the castle to keep it from falling into enemy hands (see "Developments").

Treasure

If the characters insist on tearing out the valuable control elements, they can pry loose fistfuls of emeralds, turquoise, moonstones, a huge chunk of jade, bits of amber, and large pieces of mithral, worth 10,000 gp total.

This destroys the castle's ability to move under power, generate weather effects, and so on. The castle will drift on powerful winds that carry it northward, where it ultimately crashes on the Miklos Glacier in the Spine of the World Mountains. Repairing the control mechanism requires a long period of extremely difficult and expensive work, though a *wish* spell could accomplish it.

Developments

The castle might crash, depending on the actions of the characters and various NPCs.

Crashed by Blagothkus. If the cloud giant is slain, his wife's spirit in the steering chamber is replaced by his spirit. Enraged, he avenges his death by moving the castle northward and then commanding it to crash in the Spine of the World, near the Miklos Glacier. More details of this crash and its consequences are provided in *The Rise of Tiamat.*

If the dragon is slain and the cultists are routed, Rath Modar gathers any remaining forces allied with the cult and slays Blagothkus, knowing full well that the cloud giant's death will cause the castle to crash (see above). Rath Modar then uses his *fly* spell to escape.

Characters Seize the Castle. If the adventurers befriend Blagothkus and drive off the cultists and the dragon, they may fly it anywhere, though they will certainly attract hostile attention from any dragon. If they are still aboard the castle, Rath Modar and the vampire do their utmost to thwart them.

If he remains in control of the castle, Blagothkus decides to visit the giants. He sends Skyreach Castle north to near the Spine of the World.

20. Ogre Barracks

Read the following text if the characters surprise this chamber's occupants.

> This unfurnished chamber contains a horde of ogres sleeping on piles of fur.

Unless they are drawn elsewhere by an alarm or some other disturbance, twelve **ogres** sleep on the furs heaped about this otherwise featureless structure.

Treasure

The ogres all keep small amounts of gold and silver in pouches, sacks, and chests. If the characters spend 30 minutes searching the barracks, they find 800 sp and 300 gp.

If one member of the party succeeds at a DC 20 Intelligence (Investigate) check, he or she finds a single pale blue sapphire worth 500 gp wedged into a crevice.

Developments

If any ogres are taken prisoner, charmed, or fast-talked, the characters learn relatively little. They serve the cloud giant Blagothkus (whose wife was slain some years ago), they know that the cloud giant has several guests, including "duh wizard in red robes" (Rath Modar), "duh dragon lady" (Rezmir), and "a big white dragon dat lives in duh caves" (Glazhael). Getting more than the basic rundown takes a DC 19 Charisma (Persuasion) check for each of the following three additional items:

- A vampire watches the Skyreach Castle at night. It sometimes feeds on the ogres, to their chagrin.
- The cult uses the castle to visit important sites without roads or portals. The ogres don't really know where they are other than "the green forests" and "that stretch of the moors" and "the old mountains."

- The castle's mists and navigation are all controlled by the cloud giant's magic. Without him, the castle won't fly.

The last point is untrue, but it's what Blagothkus told his ogres, and they believe him.

21. ESCLAROTTA'S TOMB

This icy cyst has no obvious means of entry or egress. However, a creature can teleport to this buried chamber via area 17.

> You appear in an oval cave carved from solid glacial ice, with no passages leading out. The ceiling is 30 feet high and lined with icicles, and bits of broken ice surround a massive white marble sarcophagus situated in the middle of the floor. The lid of the sarcophagus is sculpted into the likeness of a female giant with long flowing hair.

The sarcophagus is 20 feet long, 10 feet wide, and 10 feet tall. Dwarvish runes carved into its base spell the name ESCLAROTTA. The lid of the sarcophagus requires a DC 30 Strength check to push aside, and the bones of Blagothkus's deceased cloud giant wife are contained within. There is no treasure buried with her.

A creature in this tomb that speaks the name "Blagothkus" is instantly teleported to the ground floor of area 17.

22. CLOUD GIANT TOWER

This 70-foot-tall tower has a parapet rooftop, two unlocked doors at ground level, and no windows. The tower interior is split into two levels, each with a 30-foot-high ceiling. A staircase of chiseled ice hugs the interior wall, connecting both levels.

Unless the characters take strides to conceal their approach, the ogres on the roof spot them.

TOWER ROOFTOP

Three **ogres** guard the tower rooftop, which is furnished with a ballista. See area 6B for details.

GROUND FLOOR

A silver chime attached to the inside of each door rings whenever the door is opened, alerting the tower's inhabitants.

A staircase hugs the interior wall of this chamber, leading up to a landing with a door. The room itself contains sturdy wood-carved furnishings of giant pro-portions, including a table surrounded by four chairs. The walls are sculpted with ice murals depicting an army of hill, frost, fire, stone, and cloud giants.

Four **ogres** guard the lower level. They wear fancy plumed helmets to signify that they are members of Blagothkus's "honor guard." This simple reward keeps the ogres alert and loyal, for they know the giant could give their helms away to someone else at any time.

UPPER FLOOR

If the ogres above or below him sound the alarm, Blag-othkus cannot be surprised.

> The walls of this room are sculpted with icy murals depicting cloud giants riding giant birds. An enormous bed with a headboard of ice sculpted to resemble clouds dominates the room. Bear furs are heaped upon the bed, and two large wooden chests rest at the bed's foot.
> A blue-skinned giant sits on the floor with his legs crossed while two ogres comb his snowy white hair. The giant's hulking morningstar leans against the bed within arm's reach.

Blagothkus (appendix B) and the two **ogres** (his stewards) aren't the only inhabitants of this room. As a bonus action on his turn, Blagothkus can summon an **air elemental** that's been magically bound to the room. The elemental follows the giant's commands but cannot leave the room. It remains until dismissed by its master.

The dim-witted ogre stewards are poor conversation-alists, but Blagothkus uses them as sounding boards, expressing his concerns that the Cult of the Dragon might try to seize control of the castle. The ogres offer no advice. Clever characters can sow discord by preying on the giant's fears (see "Negotiating with the Cloud Giant" near the beginning of the episode). An alarm or the characters' sudden appearance startles him, and he reaches for his weapon. If the characters are pretending to be cultists, Blagothkus is furious at their intrusion but does not attack unless they further provoke him. The ogres defend their master to the death.

TREASURE

The chests are unlocked and loaded with silver and gold coins (12,000 gp total). One of the chests also contains a *bag of holding*, and bars of solid gold (4,000 gp worth) and silver (another 4,000 gp).

DEVELOPMENTS

If the characters surrender to Blagothkus, he asks about their names, allegiances, and plans. If the char-acters represent themselves as enemies of the cult, the giant says, "I can take care of them. But just in case, you should know that they are entirely serious about making dragons a power along the coast again. Can you imagine? The nerve." If they sway the giant to their side, he locks himself in area 19 and guides the castle northward while the characters deal with the cultists and the white dragon. Blagothkus's ultimate destination is described in *The Rise of Tiamat*.

If anyone attempts to wrest the castle from him, Blag-othkus goes to the steering tower and tries to crash the castle in the Spine of the World; see area 19 for details. If Blagothkus is killed, his spirit takes over the castle, with the same end result.

23. GIANT GUEST CHAMBERS

These rooms are set aside for giant-sized guests and have furnishings of the appropriate size.

Vanishing Wall of Ice. In each room, a large section of the outer wall vanishes for 1 minute when touched, revealing a icy landing platform. Long ago, giants would use these platforms to land their flying roc mounts.

24. Servant Barracks

Twenty **kobolds** are trying to sleep here on dozens of small piles of bedding, fur, and clothes. They are exhausted and ignore the characters unless they are in great danger. They have no treasure.

Characters questioning the kobold servants may make a DC 12 Charisma (Persuasion) check. If the characters are dressed as cultists and are fairly convincing, no check is required.

Each success brings one of the following bits of information to light; the first failure by any character means that the kobolds unite in their terror of the cultists and go completely silent. If questioned further, they start screaming for help and babbling for mercy: completely useless.

- An elf vampire lives in the crumbling tower (area 18).
- Blagothkus still speaks to his dead wife, and her spirit is the castle's pilot and protector. If the giant dies, all the magic of the castle will be undone.
- The human dragon-cult people don't really understand dragons the way that kobolds do. Dragons are fine creatures, but grumpy. They say the treasure here is for the queen of all dragons, to keep her from being grumpy.
- A red-robed wizard is working with the cultists, and his room (area 12) is off limits to all kobolds.
- The white dragon Cloudchaser loves frozen meat. Toss it into the cavern (area 25) and run!

25. Main Vault

The icy "core" of the castle is hollowed out with tunnels that break the surface at multiple points. The white dragon, Glazhael the Cloudchaser, enters and leaves via a wide funnel-shaped passageway that narrows as it draws closer to the main vault, where the Cult of the Dragon stores its treasure.

If the characters explore the tunnels, read or paraphrase the following:

> The walls of blue ice are partly transparent, revealing various things embedded in the ice all around, including coins, helmets, livestock, a handful of kobolds, and an ogre or two. Frost coats the tunnel floors and crunches underfoot.

When the characters reach the main vault, read:

> All tunnels seem to lead to a central core—a glittering cavern of ice with jagged walls and icicles the size of stalactites. This grand vault is split into two levels: an egg-shaped upper level with a sheer ledge overlooking a sunken level 30 feet below, where a massive pile of treasure rests beneath an icy glaze. Clinging to the ceiling above the hoard, wings tucked in tight along its sides with claws gripping the ice, is a huge white dragon.

Glazhael is an **adult white dragon** that is doing his part to ensure the rise of Tiamat, hopeful that the queen of evil dragons will reward him with untold power. He is, however, a bit on the dim side, thinking of visitors as either servants (who bring him food) or as enemies (who do not bring him food). Mostly, Glazhael is proud to guard this treasure for Tiamat, his most glorious and perfect queen. He rarely talks to any cultists other than Talis and is suspicious of Rezmir and the others.

If the characters speak with Glazhael, he responds with a pompous speech about the superiority of dragons over humans, dwarves, and so forth.

BLAGOTHKUS

If the characters flatter him to a ludicrous degree, he listens to anything that sounds like fawning, servile, helpful obedience but offers nothing in return. He will generously spare the lives of those who offer him tribute in the form of treasure or food. Those who challenge him become targets of his breath weapon.

When fighting, Glazhael clings to the ceiling whenever possible, using his breath weapon and Frightful Presence to start. If that doesn't scare the characters off, he makes melee attacks until his breath weapon recharges. If dropped to fewer than 40 hit points, he flees. He can navigate even the narrow tunnels by tucking in his wings. Once outside, he alerts the rest of the castle, shouting "They're after the treasure!" in Draconic.

Clever characters can lure the dragon into a narrow tunnel where it is unable to maneuver effectively. Under such circumstances, the dragon has disadvantage on its melee attacks.

TREASURE

When the characters investigate the hoard, read:

> The floor of the cavern is carpeted in gold, silver, copper, and jewels, all sealed under a sheet of ice. Dozens of old human skulls and bones are also frozen in the ice.

The treasure hoard is frozen in ice, and it requires either several fire spells or a long wait with bonfires to melt the ice. The hoard includes 500,000 cp, 100,000 sp, and 5,000 gp, a frozen chest containing 800 pp and 21 small blue sapphires worth 300 gp each, a frozen *potion of gaseous form*, a *+1 longsword*, a *+1 longbow*, *+1 leather armor*, and *bracers of defense*.

DEVELOPMENTS

If the dragon is slain, the cultists are enraged and seek immediate vengeance. The major cult players on Skyreach Castle will call out the ogres, wake the vampire, and ask the Red Wizards to find the intruders. If the characters are still around after the dragon is slain, the entire castle is on high alert until they are found and killed.

CONCLUDING THE ADVENTURE

The crash or capture of Skyreach Castle marks the end of *Hoard of the Dragon Queen*. If you are using the milestone experience rule, the characters reach 8th level for completing the adventure. By uncovering the cult's plans and hijacking a huge hoard of treasure, the characters have slowed and damaged the cult's chances of success. They may also have slain or captured important leaders of the Cult of the Dragon. But there is much more to come. The cult moves forward with its plan to free their five-headed queen out of the Nine Hells, and the mere loss of wealth will not stop the true fanatics.

The Rise of Tiamat expands on the final drive to destroy the Cult of the Dragon, and it requires great new powers and new courage. Things grow much more dangerous for the adventurers as they seek help in strange places, from the Sea of Moving Ice to the depths of the Serpent Hills. They might find a great weapon among the giants or uncover an unexpected ally within the cult itself.

Unless the characters press on, the Queen of Dragons might yet establish her personal rule over the lands of lesser creatures. The stakes are high when the gates to the Nine Hells open, and scaly doom comes out of its lair, full of fire and fangs.

The conflict reaches its apex at the Well of Dragons, where the characters and their hard-won allies face Tiamat and her greatest minions in a fight to the death!

MASK OF THE DRAGON QUEEN

APPENDIX A: BACKGROUNDS

This appendix provides players with an easy way to create characters with compelling ties to the events of *Hoard of the Dragon Queen*.

BACKGROUND TEMPLATE

Below is a background template that applies to any background that you select or create. You can replace or augment some or all of the options in your chosen background with one or more of the elements given below. Each section tells you whether it replaces or adds to your background.

THE STORY THUS FAR . . .

As the Cult of the Dragon has grown bolder, its actions have drawn attention. Your character has stumbled into the cult's scheme in some manner or has a connection to dragons. The following table provides bonds tailored to this campaign. Use them in place of or in addition to the ones you selected from (or created for) your background.

BOND (D10)

1. Leosin Erlanthar, a wandering monk, once saved your life. He's sent urgent word for you to meet him in a small town called Greenest. Looks like it's time to pay off that debt.
2. When an orc raid drove your family from your home, the people of Greenest took you in. Anyone who threatens Greenest is your sworn enemy.
3. Every five nights, you have a strange sequence of apocalyptic dreams. The world is destroyed by cold, choking fumes, lightning storms, waves of acid, and horrible fire. Each time, the dream ends with ten evil eyes glaring at you from the darkness. You feel a strange compulsion to travel to Greenest. Perhaps the answer to the riddle of your dreams awaits you there.
4. Ontharr Frume, a crusading warrior and champion of good, is your friend and mentor. He has asked you to travel to Greenest in search of rumors of increasing dragon activity.
5. You have heard rumors that your close childhood friend, a half-elf named Talis, has been kidnapped by a strange group of dragon cultists. Your investigations into the cult have led you to the town of Greenest. You must save her!
6. Being the grandchild of a renowned dragon slayer is usually a good way to impress people, but just last week a gang of ruffians attack you. You barely escaped with your life, but as you fled, the ruffians told you that the Cult of the Dragon never forgets and always avenges. You're hoping to lie low in a sleepy little town called Greenest until this blows over.
7. On his deathbed, your father confessed that he had become involved with a group called the Cult of the Dragon. They paid him to smuggle goods across the Sword Coast. Wracked by guilt, he begged you to investigate the cult and undo the evil he may have helped foster. He urged you to begin your search in a town called Greenest.

8. The dragons destroyed everything you hold dear. They killed your family and destroyed your home. Now, with nothing but what you carry on your back and a horrid scar of the near fatal wounds you sustained in the attack, you seek revenge.
9. You and your family were members of the Cult of the Dragon, until your rivals in the cult arranged to wipe you out. Though they slaughtered your kin, you survived, but they think you're dead. Now is your chance for vengeance! Your hit list consists of three names: a human cultist named Frulam Mondath, a half-orc named Bog Luck, and a half-dragon named Rezmir. You have arrived in Greenest, knowing it's next on the cult's list of targets.
10. You have a secret. You once were a gold dragon who served Bahamut. You were too proud and vain, to the point that Bahamut decided to teach you a lesson. You have been trapped in a weak, humanoid body, with your memories of your former life but a dim shadow. You remember only one thing with perfect clarity: Bahamut's command to go into the world and prove your devotion to the cause of good. If you prove worthy, on your death you will return to his side in your true form.

OPTIONAL FEATURES

Below are two optional features that you can choose in place of the feature normally granted by your background.

FEATURE: CULT OF THE DRAGON INFILTRATOR

You have infiltrated the ranks of the Cult of the Dragon. Having spied on the organization for quite some time, you are familiar with its inner workings and customs. You have a second identity as an initiate of the cult, enough of a facade to blend in as a simple grunt or servant.

FEATURE: DRAGON SCHOLAR

You have studied dragons and their lore for many years. You can automatically identify locations built or used by dragons and can identify dragon eggs and scales by sight. If you fail an Intelligence check to recall lore relating to dragons, you know someone or some book you can consult for the answer unless the DM rules that the lore is unknown.

APPENDIX B: MONSTERS

AMBUSH DRAKE
Medium dragon, unaligned

Armor Class 13 (natural armor)
Hit Points 22 (4d6 + 8)
Speed 30 ft.

STR	DEX	CON	INT	WIS	CHA
13 (+1)	15 (+2)	14 (+2)	4 (–3)	11 (+0)	6 (–2)

Skills Perception +4, Stealth +4
Damage Resistances poison
Senses darkvision 60 ft., passive Perception 14
Languages understands Draconic but can't speak it
Challenge 1/2 (100 XP)

Pack Tactics. The drake has advantage on an attack roll against a creature if at least one of the drake's allies is within 5 feet of the creature and the ally isn't incapacitated.

Surprise Attack. If the drake surprises a creature and hits it with an attack during the first round of combat, the target takes an extra 7 (2d6) damage from the attack.

ACTIONS

Bite. *Melee Weapon Attack:* +4 to hit, reach 5 ft., one target. *Hit:* 4 (1d6 + 1) piercing damage.

AZBARA JOS
Medium humanoid (human), lawful evil

Armor Class 13 (16 with *mage armor*)
Hit Points 39 (6d8 + 12)
Speed 30 ft.

STR	DEX	CON	INT	WIS	CHA
9 (–1)	16 (+3)	14 (+2)	16 (+3)	13 (+1)	11 (+0)

Saving Throws Int +5, Wis +3
Skills Arcana +5, Deception +2, Insight +3, Stealth +5
Senses passive Perception 11
Languages Common, Draconic, Infernal, Primordial, Thayan
Challenge 4 (1,100)

Special Equipment. Azbara has two scrolls of *mage armor*.

Potent Cantrips. When Azbara casts an evocation cantrip and misses, or the target succeeds on its saving throw, the target still takes half the cantrip's damage but suffers no other effect.

Sculpt Spells. When Azbara casts an evocation spell that affects other creatures that he can see, he can choose a number of them equal to 1 + the spell's level to succeed on their saving throws against the spell. Those creatures take no damage if they would normally take half damage from the spell.

Spellcasting. Azbara is a 6th-level spellcaster that uses Intelligence as his spellcasting ability (spell save DC 13, +5 to hit with spell attacks). Azbara has the following spells prepared from the wizard spell list:

Cantrips (at will): *mage hand, prestidigitation, ray of frost, shocking grasp*
1st level (4 slots): *fog cloud, magic missile, shield, thunderwave*
2nd level (3 slots): *invisibility, misty step, scorching ray*
3rd level (3 slots): *counterspell, dispel magic, fireball*

ACTIONS

Dagger. *Melee or Ranged Weapon Attack:* +5 to hit, reach 5 ft. or ranged 20 ft./60 ft., one target. *Hit:* 5 (1d4 + 3) piercing damage.

AMBUSH DRAKE

Blagothkus

Huge giant (cloud giant), neutral evil

Armor Class 17 (splint)
Hit Points 138 (12d12 + 60)
Speed 40 ft.

STR	DEX	CON	INT	WIS	CHA
26 (+8)	13 (+1)	20 (+5)	16 (+3)	15 (+2)	15 (+2)

Saving Throws Con +9, Wis +6, Cha +6
Skills Arcana +7, Insight +6, Intimidation +6, Perception +6
Senses passive Perception 16
Languages Common, Draconic, Giant
Challenge 9 (5,000 XP)

Keen Smell. Blagothkus has advantage on Wisdom (Perception) checks that rely on smell.

Innate Spellcasting. Blagothkus can innately cast the following spells (spell save DC 15), requiring no material components:

3/day each: *fog cloud, levitate*

Spellcasting. Blagothkus is a 5th-level spellcaster that uses Intelligence as his spellcasting ability (spell save DC 15, +7 to hit with spell attacks). Blagothkus has the following spells prepared from the wizard spell list:

Cantrips (at will): *light, mage hand, prestidigitation*
1st level (4 slots): *detect magic, identify, magic missile, shield*
2nd level (3 slots): *gust of wind, misty step, shatter*
3rd level (2 slots): *fly, lightning bolt*

Actions

Multiattack. Blagothkus attacks twice with his morningstar.

Morningstar. *Melee Weapon Attack:* +10 to hit, reach 10 ft., one target. *Hit:* 21 (3d8 + 8) piercing damage.

Captain Othelstan

Medium humanoid (human), lawful evil

Armor Class 19 (splint, shield)
Hit Points 93 (11d10 + 33)
Speed 30 ft.

STR	DEX	CON	INT	WIS	CHA
19 (+4)	10 (+0)	16 (+3)	13 (+1)	14 (+2)	12 (+1)

Saving Throws Str +7, Con +6
Skills Athletics +7, Intimidation +4, Perception +5, Religion +4
Senses passive Perception 15
Languages Common, Draconic, Giant
Challenge 5 (1,800)

Action Surge (Recharges when Othelstan Finishes a Short or Long Rest). On his turn, Othelstan can take one additional action.

Tiamat's Blessing of Retribution. When Othelstan takes damage that reduces him to 0 hit points, he immediately regains 20 hit points. If he has 20 hit points or fewer at the end of his next turn, he dies.

Actions

Multiattack. Othelstan attacks twice with his flail or spear, or makes two ranged attacks with his spears.

Flail. *Melee Weapon Attack:* +7 to hit, reach 5 ft., one target. *Hit:* 8 (1d8 + 4) bludgeoning damage.

Spear. *Melee or Ranged Weapon Attack:* +7 to hit, reach 5 ft. or ranged 20 ft./60 ft., one target. *Hit:* 7 (1d6 + 4) piercing damage.

Dragonclaw

Medium humanoid (human), neutral evil

Armor Class 14 (leather armor)
Hit Points 16 (3d8 + 3)
Speed 30 ft.

STR	DEX	CON	INT	WIS	CHA
9 (−1)	16 (+3)	13 (+1)	11 (+0)	10 (+0)	12 (+1)

Saving Throws Wis +2
Skills Deception +3, Stealth +5
Senses passive Perception 10
Languages Common, Draconic
Challenge 1 (200 XP)

Dragon Fanatic. The dragonclaw has advantage on saving throws against being charmed or frightened. While the dragonclaw can see a dragon or higher-ranking Cult of the Dragon cultist friendly to it, the dragonclaw ignores the effects of being charmed or frightened.

Fanatical Advantage. Once per turn, if the dragonclaw makes a weapon attack with advantage on the attack roll and hits, it deals an extra 7 (2d6) damage.

Pack Tactics. The dragonclaw has advantage on an attack roll against a creature if at least one of the dragonclaw's allies is within 5 feet of the creature and the ally isn't incapacitated.

Actions

Multiattack. The dragonclaw attacks twice with its scimitar.

Scimitar. *Melee Weapon Attack:* +5 to hit, reach 5 ft., one target. *Hit:* 6 (1d6 + 3) slashing damage.

> ### Dragonwing
>
> A dragonwing uses the dragonclaw stat block except that it has double the normal hit points, double the normal hit dice, and is Challenge Rating 2 (450 XP). A more detailed statistics block for the dragonwing will appear in *The Rise of Tiamat*.

Dralmorrer Borngray

Medium humanoid (high-elf), neutral evil

Armor Class 16 (studded leather armor, shield)
Hit Points 52 (7d10 + 14)
Speed 30 ft.

STR	DEX	CON	INT	WIS	CHA
18 (+4)	14 (+2)	14 (+2)	16 (+3)	10 (+0)	8 (−1)

Saving Throws Str +6, Con +4
Skills Arcana +5, Deception +1, Insight +2, Perception +2, Religion +5
Senses darkvision 60 ft., passive Perception 12
Languages Common, Bullywug, Draconic, Elvish, Goblin, Sylvan
Challenge 3 (700 XP)

DRALMORRER BORNGRAY

Fey Ancestry. Dralmorrer has advantage on saving throws against being charmed, and magic can't put him to sleep.

Spellcasting. Dralmorrer is a 7th-level spellcaster that uses Intelligence as his spellcasting ability (spell save DC 13, +5 to hit with spell attacks). Dralmorrer has the following spells prepared from the wizard spell list:

Cantrips (at will): *fire bolt, prestidigitation, shocking grasp*
1st level (4 slots): *longstrider, magic missile, shield, thunderwave*
2nd level (2 slots): *magic weapon, misty step*

War Magic. When Dralmorrer uses his action to cast a cantrip, he can also take a bonus action to make one weapon attack.

Weapon Bond. Provided his longsword is on the same plane, Dralmorrer can take a bonus action to teleport it to his hand.

Actions

Multiattack. Dralmorrer attacks twice, either with his longsword or dagger.

Longsword. *Melee Weapon Attack:* +6 to hit, reach 5 ft., one target. *Hit:* 8 (1d8 + 4) slashing damage.

Dagger. *Melee or Ranged Weapon Attack:* +6 to hit, reach 5 ft. or ranged 20 ft./60 ft., one target. *Hit:* 6 (1d4 + 4) piercing damage.

Frulam Mondath

Medium humanoid (human), lawful evil

Armor Class 16 (chain mail)
Hit Points 44 (8d8 + 8)
Speed 30 ft.

STR	DEX	CON	INT	WIS	CHA
14 (+2)	10 (+0)	13 (+1)	11 (+0)	18 (+4)	15 (+2)

Saving Throws Wis +6, Cha +4
Skills Deception +4, History +2, Religion +2
Senses passive Perception 14
Languages Common, Draconic, Infernal
Challenge 2 (450 XP)

Spellcasting. Frulam is a 5th-level spellcaster that uses Wisdom as her spellcasting ability (spell save DC 14, +6 to hit with spell attacks). Frulam has the following spells prepared from the cleric spell list:

Cantrips (at will): *light, sacred flame, thaumaturgy*
1st level (4 slots): *command, cure wounds, healing word, sanctuary*
2nd level (3 slots): *calm emotions, hold person, spiritual weapon*
3rd level (2 slots): *mass healing word, spirit guardians*

Actions

Multiattack. Frulam attacks twice with her halberd.

Halberd. *Melee Weapon Attack:* +5 to hit, reach 10 ft., one target. *Hit:* 7 (1d10 + 2) bludgeoning damage.

GUARD DRAKE

Medium dragon, unaligned

Armor Class 14 (natural armor)
Hit Points 52 (7d8 + 21)
Speed 30 ft.

STR	DEX	CON	INT	WIS	CHA
16 (+3)	11 (+0)	16 (+3)	4 (−3)	10 (+0)	7 (−2)

Skills Perception +2
Damage Resistances lightning
Senses darkvision 60 ft., passive Perception 12
Languages understands Draconic but can't speak it
Challenge 2 (450 XP)

ACTIONS

Multiattack. The drake attacks twice, once with its bite and once with its tail.

Bite. *Melee Weapon Attack:* +5 to hit, reach 5 ft., one target. *Hit:* 7 (1d8 + 3) piercing damage.

Tail. *Melee Weapon Attack:* +5 to hit, reach 5 ft., one target. *Hit:* 6 (1d6 + 3) bludgeoning damage.

JAMNA GLEAMSILVER

Small humanoid (gnome), neutral

Armor Class 15 (leather armor)
Hit Points 22 (4d6 + 8)
Speed 25 ft.

STR	DEX	CON	INT	WIS	CHA
8 (−1)	17 (+3)	14 (+2)	15 (+2)	10 (+0)	12 (+1)

Saving Throws Dex +5, Int +4
Skills Acrobatics +5, Deception +3, Insight +2, Perception +4, Persuasion +3, Stealth +7
Senses darkvision 60 ft., passive Perception 14
Languages Common, Gnomish, Goblin, Sylvan
Challenge 1 (200 XP)

Cunning Action. Jamna can take a bonus action to take the Dash, Disengage, or Hide action.

Gnome Cunning. Jamna has advantage on Intelligence, Wisdom, and Charisma saving throws against magic.

Spellcasting. Jamna is a 4th-level spellcaster that uses Intelligence as her spellcasting ability (spell save DC 12, +4 to hit with spell attacks). Jamna has the following spells prepared from the wizard spell list:

Cantrips (at will): *mage hand, minor illusion, prestidigitation, ray of frost*
1st level (3 slots): *charm person, color spray, disguise self, longstrider*

ACTIONS

Multiattack. Jamna attacks twice with her shortswords.

Shortsword. *Melee Weapon Attack:* +5 to hit, reach 5 ft., one target. *Hit:* 6 (1d6 + 3) piercing damage, or 9 (1d6 + 3 plus 1d6) piercing damage if the target is Medium or larger.

LANGDEDROSA CYANWRATH

Medium humanoid (half-dragon), lawful evil

Armor Class 17 (splint)
Hit Points 57 (6d12 + 18)
Speed 30 ft.

STR	DEX	CON	INT	WIS	CHA
19 (+4)	13 (+1)	16 (+3)	10 (+0)	14 (+2)	12 (+1)

Saving Throws Str +6, Con +5
Skills Athletics +6, Intimidation +3, Perception +4
Damage Resistances lightning
Senses blindsight 10 ft., darkvision 60 ft., passive Perception 14
Languages Common, Draconic
Challenge 4 (1,100 XP)

Action Surge (Recharges when Langdedrosa Finishes a Short or Long Rest). On his turn, Langdedrosa can take one additional action.

Improved Critical. Langdedrosa's weapon attacks score a critical hit on a roll of 19 or 20.

ACTIONS

Multiattack. Langdedrosa attacks twice, either with his greatsword or spear.

Greatsword. *Melee Weapon Attack:* +6 to hit, reach 5 ft., one target. *Hit:* 11 (2d6 + 4) slashing damage.

Spear. *Melee or Ranged Weapon Attack:* +6 to hit, reach 5 ft. or ranged 20 ft./60 ft., one target. *Hit:* 7 (1d6 + 4) piercing damage.

Lightning Breath (Recharge 5–6). Langdedrosa breathes lightning in a 30-foot line that is 5 feet wide. Each creature in the line must make a DC 13 Dexterity saving throw, taking 22 (4d10) lightning damage on a failed save, or half as much damage on a successful one.

PHARBLEX SPATTERGOO

Medium humanoid (bullywug), chaotic evil

Armor Class 15 (studded leather armor, shield)
Hit Points 59 (7d8 + 28)
Speed 20 ft., swim 40 ft.

STR	DEX	CON	INT	WIS	CHA
15 (+2)	12 (+1)	18 (+4)	11 (+0)	16 (+3)	7 (−2)

Saving Throws Str +4, Con +6
Skills Perception +5, Religion +2, Stealth +3
Senses passive Perception 15
Languages Common, Bullywug
Challenge 3 (700 XP)

Amphibious. Pharblex can breathe air and water.

Poison Strike (3/Day). Once per turn, when Pharblex hits with a melee attack, he can expend a use of this trait to deal an extra 9 (2d8) poison damage.

Spellcasting. Pharblex is a 6th-level spellcaster that uses Wisdom as his spellcasting ability (spell save DC 13, +5 to hit with spell attacks). Pharblex has the following spells prepared from the druid spell list:

Cantrips (at will): *druidcraft, guidance, poison cloud*
1st level (4 slots): *cure wounds, entangle, healing word, thunderwave*
2nd level (3 slots): *barkskin, beast sense, spike growth*
3rd level (3 slots): *plant growth, water walk*

Standing Leap. As part of his movement and without a running start, Pharblex can long jump up to 20 feet and high jump up to 10 feet.

Swamp Camouflage. Pharblex has advantage on Dexterity (Stealth) checks made to hide in swampy terrain.

ACTIONS

Multiattack. Pharblex attacks twice, once with his bite and once with his spear.

Bite. *Melee Weapon Attack:* +5 to hit, reach 5 ft., one target. *Hit:* 4 (1d4 + 2) piercing damage.

Spear. *Melee or Ranged Weapon Attack:* +5 to hit, reach 5 ft. or ranged 20 ft./60 ft., one target. *Hit:* 5 (1d6 + 2) piercing damage.

RATH MODAR

Medium humanoid (human), lawful evil

Armor Class 13 (16 with *mage armor*)
Hit Points 71 (11d8 + 22)
Speed 30 ft.

STR	DEX	CON	INT	WIS	CHA
11 (+0)	16 (+3)	14 (+2)	18 (+4)	14 (+2)	10 (+0)

Saving Throws Int +7, Wis +5
Skills Arcana +7, Deception +3, Insight +5, Stealth +6
Senses passive Perception 12
Languages Common, Draconic, Infernal, Primordial, Thayan
Challenge 6 (2,300 XP)

Special Equipment. Rath has a *staff of fire*, and scrolls of *dimension door, feather fall,* and *fireball.*

Spellcasting. Rath is an 11th-level spellcaster who uses Intelligence as his spellcasting ability (spell save DC 15, +7 to hit with spell attacks). Rath has the following spells prepared from the wizard spell list:

Cantrips (at will): *fire bolt, minor illusion, prestidigitation, shocking grasp*
1st level (4 slots): *chromatic orb, color spray, mage armor, magic missile*
2nd level (3 slots): *detect thoughts, mirror image, phantasmal force*
3rd level (3 slots): *counterspell, fireball, major image*
4th level (3 slots): *confusion, greater invisibility*
5th level (2 slots): *mislead, seeming*
6th level (1 slot): *globe of invulnerability*

RATH MODAR

ACTIONS

Quarterstaff. *Melee Weapon Attack:* +4 to hit, reach 5 ft., one target. *Hit:* 4 (1d8) bludgeoning damage.

REACTIONS

Illusory Self (Recharges when Rath Finishes a Short or Long Rest). When a creature Rath can see makes an attack roll against him, he can interpose an illusory duplicate between the attacker and him. The attack automatically misses Rath, then the illusion dissipates.

REZMIR

Medium humanoid (half-black dragon), neutral evil

Armor Class 13 (15 with the *Black Dragon Mask*)
Hit Points 90 (12d8 + 36)
Speed 30 ft.

STR	DEX	CON	INT	WIS	CHA
18 (+4)	16 (+3)	16 (+3)	15 (+2)	12 (+1)	14 (+2)

Saving Throws Dex +6, Wis +4
Skills Arcana +5, Stealth +9
Damage Immunities acid
Condition Immunities charmed, frightened
Senses blindsight 10 ft., darkvision 120 ft., passive Perception 11
Languages Common, Draconic, Infernal, Giant, Netherese
Challenge 7 (2,900 XP)

Special Equipment. Rezmir has the *Black Dragon Mask*, *Hazirawn*, and an *insignia of claws* (see appendix C for all items).

Amphibious. Rezmir can breathe air and water.

Dark Advantage. Once per turn, Rezmir can deal an extra 10 (3d6) damage when she hits with a weapon attack, provided Rezmir has advantage on the attack roll.

Draconic Majesty. While wearing no armor and wearing the *Black Dragon Mask*, Rezmir adds her Charisma bonus to her AC (included).

Immolation. When Rezmir is reduced to 0 hit points, her body disintegrates into a pile of ash.

Legendary Resistance (1/Day). If Rezmir fails a saving throw while wearing the *Black Dragon Mask*, she can choose to succeed instead.

ACTIONS

Greatsword (Hazirawn). *Melee Weapon Attack:* +9 to hit, reach 5 ft., one target. *Hit:* 13 (2d6 + 6) slashing damage plus 7 (2d6) necrotic damage. If the target is a creature, it can't regain hit points for 1 minute. The target can make a DC 15 Constitution saving throw at the end of each of its turns, ending this effect early on a success.

Caustic Bolt. *Ranged Spell Attack:* +8 to hit, range 90 ft., one target. *Hit:* 18 (4d8) acid damage.

Acid Breath (Recharge 5–6). Rezmir breathes acid in a 30-foot line that is 5 feet wide. Each creature in the line must make a DC 14 Dexterity saving throw, taking 22 (5d8) acid damage on a failed save, or half as much damage on a successful one.

LEGENDARY ACTIONS

If she is wearing the *Black Dragon Mask*, Rezmir can take up to two legendary actions between each of her turns, taking the actions all at once or spreading them over the round. A legendary action can be taken only at the start or end of a turn. Rezmir has the following legendary action options, some of which expend more than one action when taken:

2 Actions. A 15-foot radius of magical darkness extends from a point Rezmir can see within 60 feet of her and spreads around corners. The darkness lasts as long as Rezmir maintains concentration, up to 1 minute. A creature with darkvision can't see through this darkness, and no natural light can illuminate it. If any of the area overlaps with an area of light created by a spell of 2nd level or lower, the spell creating the light is dispelled.

1 Action. Rezmir makes one melee attack.

1 Action. Rezmir takes the Hide action.

TALIS THE WHITE

Medium humanoid (half-elf), lawful evil

Armor Class 18 (*+1 scale mail*, shield)
Hit Points 58 (9d8 + 18)
Speed 30 ft.

STR	DEX	CON	INT	WIS	CHA
14 (+2)	12 (+1)	14 (+2)	10 (+0)	16 (+3)	16 (+3)

Saving Throws Wis +6, Cha +6
Skills Deception +6, Insight +6, Perception +6, Persuasion +6
Senses darkvision 60 ft., passive Perception 16
Languages Common, Draconic, Elvish, Infernal
Challenge 5 (1,800 XP)

Special Equipment. Talis has *+1 scale mail* and a *wand of winter* (see appendix C).

Fey Ancestry. Talis has advantage on saving throws against being charmed, and magic can't put her to sleep.

Spellcasting. Talis is a 9th-level spellcaster that uses Wisdom as her spellcasting ability (spell save DC 14, +6 to hit with spell attacks). Talis has the following spells prepared from the cleric spell list:

Cantrips (at will): *guidance, resistance, thaumaturgy*
1st level (4 slots): *command, cure wounds, healing word, inflict wounds*
2nd level (3 slots): *blindness/deafness, lesser restoration, spiritual weapon* (spear)
3rd level (3 slots): *dispel magic, mass healing word, sending*
4th level (3 slots): *death ward, freedom of movement*
5th level (1 slot): *insect plague*

Winter Strike (3/Day). Once per turn, when Talis hits with a melee attack, she can expend a use of this trait to deal an extra 9 (2d8) cold damage.

ACTIONS

Spear. *Melee or Ranged Weapon Attack:* +5 to hit, reach 5 ft. or ranged 20 ft./60 ft., one target. *Hit:* 6 (1d6 + 2) piercing damage.

Appendix C: Magic Items

Black Dragon Mask
Wondrous item, legendary (requires attunement)

This horned mask of glossy ebony has horns and a skull-like mien. The mask reshapes to fit a wearer attuned to it. While you are wearing the mask and attuned to it, you can access the following properties.

Damage Absorption. You have damage resistance to acid. If you already have damage resistance to acid from another source, you gain immunity to acid damage. If you already have immunity to acid damage from another source, you regain hit points equal to half of any acid damage you are dealt.

Draconic Majesty. While you are wearing no armor, you can add your Charisma modifier to your Armor Class.

Dragon Breath. If you have a breath weapon that requires rest to recharge, it gains a recharge of 6.

Dragon Sight. You gain darkvision with a radius of 60 feet, or an additional 60 feet of darkvision if you already have that sense. Once per day, you can gain blindsight out to a range of 30 feet for 5 minutes.

Dragon Tongue. You can speak and understand Draconic. You also have advantage on any Charisma check you make against black dragons.

Legendary Resistance (1/Day). If you fail a saving throw, you can choose to succeed instead.

Water Breathing. You can breathe underwater.

Hazirawn
Weapon (greatsword), legendary (requires attunement)

A sentient (neutral evil) greatsword, *Hazirawn* is capable of speech in Common and Netherese. Even if you aren't attuned to the sword, you gain a +1 bonus on attack rolls and damage rolls made with this magic weapon. If you aren't attuned to *Hazirawn*, you deal an extra 1d6 necrotic damage when you hit with it.

Increased Potency. While you are attuned to this weapon, its bonus on attack rolls and damage rolls increases to +2, and a hit deals an extra 2d6 necrotic damage (instead of 1d6).

Spells. *Hazirawn* has 4 charges to cast spells. As long as the sword is attuned to you and you are holding it in your hand, you can cast *detect magic* (1 charge), *detect evil and good* (1 charge), or *detect thoughts* (2 charges). Each night at midnight, Hazirawn regains 1d4 expended charges.

Wounding. While you are attuned to the weapon, any creature that you hit with *Hazirawn* can't regain hit points for 1 minute. The target can make a DC 15 Constitution saving throw at the end of each of its turns, ending this effect early on a success.

Insignia of Claws
Wondrous item, uncommon

The jewels in this insignia of the Cult of the Dragon flare with purple light when you enter combat, empowering your natural fists or natural weapons.

While wearing the insignia, you gain a +1 bonus to the attack rolls and the damage rolls you make with unarmed strikes and natural weapons. Such attacks are considered to be magical.

Wand of Winter
Wand, rare (requires attunement)

This wand looks and feels like an icicle.

The wand has 7 charges, which are used to fuel the spells within it. With the wand in hand, you can use your action to cast one of the following spells from the wand, even if you are incapable of casting spells: *ray of frost* (no charges, or 1 charge to cast at 5th level; +5 to hit with ranged spell attack), *sleet storm* (3 charges; spell save DC 15), or *ice storm* (4 charges; spell save DC 15). No components are required.

The wand regains 1d6 + 1 expended charges each day at dawn. If you expend the wand's last charge, roll a d20. On a 20, the wand melts away, forever destroyed.

WAND OF WINTER

BRYAN SYME

What Happens Next?

THE ADVENTURE'S NOT OVER YET, FOR THE CULT OF THE DRAGON IS NOT SO EASILY DEFEATED. Already, the cult's remaining leaders plot to snuff out the adventurers. Meanwhile, at the Well of Dragons, the cult and its dragon allies amass. The unholy chants and roars of dragons echo through the desolation of the volcanic caldera, vowing Tiamat's return. And in the Nine Hells, Tiamat rages, demanding her followers gather more tribute before she sets foot in the Forgotten Realms. Hope remains, though, for the wind carries whispers of a great meeting of factions in Waterdeep. If such rumors are true, heroes will be needed to unite these groups against their common enemy.

Beyond this book, the *Tyranny of Dragons* story takes flight. Bring your *Tyranny of Dragons* game to life with apparel, miniatures, and D&D play accessories. In the *Tyranny of Dragons* comic, visit Baldur's Gate and discover how a young wizard schemes to prove his worth as a cult leader. In the *Neverwinter* video game, create a character to confront the Cult of the Dragon before facing the Queen of Dragons herself. And find a regular D&D game at a store near you. Learn more at **DungeonsandDragons.com**.

ALL ROADS LEAD TO AN EPIC CONFRONTATION WITH THE QUEEN OF DRAGONS AND THE CONCLUSION OF THE *TYRANNY OF DRAGONS* STORY IN *THE RISE OF TIAMAT*.